D0539246

ON THIN ICE

ON THIN ICE

Breakdowns, Whiteouts and Survival on the World's Deadliest Roads

Hugh Rowland

With Michael Lent

Unless otherwise noted, all photographs
in the insert are courtesy of the author.

Copyright © 2010 R&R Backhoe Service and Con Leche, Inc.

The right of Hugh Rowland to be identified as the author
of this work has been asserted by him in accordance with
the Copyright, Designs and Patents Act 1988.

This edition first published in Great Britain in 2010 by
Orion Books
an imprint of the Orion Publishing Group Ltd
Orion House, 5 Upper St Martin's Lane,
London WC2H 9EA
An Hachette Livre UK Company

1 3 5 7 9 10 8 6 4 2

A CIP catalogue record for this book is available
from the British Library.

ISBN: 978 1 4091 2248 7 (hardback)

Design by Sunil Manchikanti

Printed in the UK by CPI Mackays, Chatham ME5 8TD

The Orion Publishing Group's policy is to use papers that are natural,
renewable and recyclable and made from wood grown in sustainable forests.
The logging and manufacturing processes are expected to conform to
the environmental regulations of the country of origin.

Every effort has been made to fulfil requirements with regard
to reproducing copyright material. The author and publisher
will be glad to rectify any omissions at the earliest opportunity.

www.orionbooks.co.uk

*To the brave people of the Northwest Territories
who have given their blood, sweat, and tears to carve a
home out of the ice and snow. May their stories of courage
and self-reliance never be forgotten.*

THE GARY ROBINSON FUND

Established in memory of Gary Robinson, who lost his life on the ice roads, the Gary Robinson Memorial Fund provides financial support to those individuals or charitable organizations involved in search and rescue/recovery or emergency response activities. To find out more about the fund or to make a donation, visit the Yellowknife Community Foundation at www.yellowknifecommunityfoundation.ca.

ACKNOWLEDGMENTS

There are some people I'd like to thank for making this book possible. For starters, Dianne, my wife. They say that behind every good man is a good woman, and she's all of that. She has given us three wonderful children, Karly, Chandra-Jo, and Candace, who make their dad proud and always inspire me to work hard and never quit.

I'm grateful to Dan Greenberg, my agent, and Brenda Copeland, my editor.

Thanks to the History Channel folks for getting the ice road truckers story out there in the first place. Producer Dolores Gavin had the original idea of doing a show about us. It was her baby. Thanks to freelance cinematographer Gavin Brennan from the IRT, who got me to write the book. He said, "All kinds of people watch the show but from the stories you tell, they don't know the half of it." Well, now they do. Also thanks to Beth Dietrich and Lynn Gardner from the

HC. Ice road trucking is a hell of a good way to make a living and it's great that so many people know a little more about what we're doing up there in the Arctic.

Special thanks to Mike Lent for doing one hell of a good job getting all the ice road stories and my life experiences down on paper. He might not be much of a truck driver, snowmobile driver, navigator, or ice fisherman, for that matter, but he pulls his weight on the page and is pretty handy with a pen and tape recorder. He and I are grateful to Ted Heyck and David Rambo for giving Mike constant encouragement and a good place to work.

Thanks to Lynn Riedesel, who helped with transcribing hours and hours' worth of audio recordings. I'm especially grateful to my sister Terry; her husband, Clay; and their kids, Ken and Kim, for allowing us to work at their home up in Yellowknife.

As far as ice road and Hugh Rowland stories go, this is just the tip of the iceberg. I've got more than thirty years of life experiences in me.

HUGH ROWLAND

CONTENTS

FOREWORD

Forty-five below zero in a whiteout snowstorm with the ice cracking and making a nerve-jangling sound like God dropping plate-glass windows from the sky—that was my first taste of Hugh Rowland's world. Two weeks before I arrived in Yellowknife, a security guard had plunged through the ice and died within fifteen minutes. While I was there, another man froze to death. He was found completely naked. It was the lead story in the local newspaper. If you're in a blizzard, the most important thing to remember is this: Never get out of your truck. The raging storm and cold temperatures can quickly overwhelm your senses and you may become disoriented. Like the Yellowknife security guard, people caught in a blizzard are often found buck naked and frozen. Apparently there's something called paradoxical undressing, which occurs when a person is freezing and his muscles are failing. If frostbite hasn't induced him to find shelter, it's as if the brain decides to put the body out of its misery. People in the para-doxical undressing state describe having a feeling that they can't breathe anymore. Other times, they will hallucinate and imagine tropical locations or extreme warmth. In both cases, people will start tearing off their clothes. It doesn't happen every time, but it seems to be a long-dormant, last-ditch primal defense mechanism that is suddenly awakened in some people when they are in the process of freezing to death. A few have been found in time to survive their birthday-suit big freeze but it's a tough way to earn your "I survived hypothermia" T-shirt.

It was against this backdrop that I started to work with Hugh Rowland.

Hugh and I began this project in December 2008. The day before our first trek on the ice road, a fully loaded big rig slammed into a fuel truck out on a portage. The mangled wreckage was strewn on the side of a snowbank beneath a stand of evergreens. It was close enough to touch as we navi-gated past. At first, we worked by phone and e-mail. It was safer that way. Warmer, too. The following February, Hugh was waiting for the third season of *Ice Road Truckers* to be-gin and his departure to the Yukon was imminent. Not one to let the grass grow under his feet, Hugh invited me to stay in his home for eight days to get to know him; his wife, Dianne; and his family and friends like Grant, Rick, John, Jim, Cary the tattoo artist, Chickie, Diana, Rick, and Perry. They call him Hoodoo or Huge, and it is clearly a point of pride to have worked with or for Hugh Rowland. Hugh's friends and family described to me a bighearted man of hard-earned principles, who was very different from his "cocky tough guy" portrayal on television. The real Hugh Rowland is hardworking and no-nonsense, but also both a kid and a mentor at heart. His easy grace and a confidence in his own abilities draw others to him. He is shrewd in business but also give-you-the-shirt-off-his-back generous. In fact, Hugh did give me his coat when I was unable to find clothing in Southern California that could handle the rigors of the Arctic.

Hugh Rowland's prodigious appetite for challenging work and adventure is the stuff of record and legend. Over the past quarter-century, he has made more runs, carried more tonnage, and survived more close calls than any other ice road driver. Having mastered one of the world's most difficult jobs, he has lived to tell the tale.

Four weeks after the February trip, I joined Hugh on an excursion on the famed ice roads out of Yellowknife. I saw firsthand many of the things that he describes in this book. There was the bone-chilling temperature, the Arctic storms, the beauty and brutality of the landscape, crashes, both human frailty and human indomitability. The winter roads of the Arctic are a feat of modern engineering and Old World guts. Sadly, Hugh foresees an end to the ice roads within the next decade. That would make him the last of his kind. I hope he's wrong. Whatever happens, Hugh Rowland's place in the history of the Arctic winter roads is carved in ice with a jack-hammer.

MICHAEL LENT

There is a road made of snow and ice that exists only in winter, in a marvelous part of Canada so strange, so far north that hardly anybody lives there. The road forges an overland link in the Northwest Territories between two of the world's largest inland seas: Great Slave Lake, near the southern border above Alberta province, and Great Bear Lake, on the Arctic Circle. The length of the road changes each winter with all of the troubles encountered during construction, but usually runs about 325 miles, some of them a little rugged.

EDITH IGLAUER IN 1974
Denison's Ice Road

1

SNOW, WATER, AND ICE

now is 90 percent air.

If you're caught out in the bush, you'll need buckets of melted snow to get enough water to keep you alive. An entire pot of snow boiled down might only get you a few sips— that's a problem when it's 60 below zero and you're a hundred miles from the nearest person. You need a lot of energy to maintain a core body temperature and if you don't get water into you fast enough (the colder it is, the bigger the chance of severe dehydration), you'll be cashing it in and meeting your maker. Knowing the science of water, snow, ice, and freezing is critical to anybody who needs to work and survive in the Arctic—like me. I've been driving trucks on the ice roads of the Northwest Territories of Canada for more than twenty-six years, and I've been stuck out in the bush lots of times, especially in the early days, before cell phones and everything else we have now. And I'm still here.

At the end of November, when the lakes and rivers of the Arctic Circle are blanketed by deep snow, it's time to build the ice roads. These roads—you'll find them in Canada, Alaska, Russia, and Scandinavia—bear the trucks that haul machinery, concrete, steel, fuel, explosives, and basic life essentials. They're a lifeline to remote places that don't have any road access the rest of the year. Building the ice roads was perilous back in the 1950s, when John Denison invented the process. It still is. Over the years, forty men have gone through the ice roads and perished. I've known most of them.

The roads are built on top of the ice that forms naturally over lakes, rivers, and oceans. Join up one frozen body of water with another, build connector roads called portages over any land in between, and you have a road made of ice. The ice isn't strong enough to support heavy loads by itself, though; it has to be thickened by smashing down the snow and knocking the air out of it. That's the first step. But snow is full of air and is a world-class insulator for anything that's underneath, so after you beat it down, you have to plow it away to expose the ice below it to the wind and chilling Arctic air. The ice will freeze from the bottom up and thicken until it's strong enough to hold up a truck loaded down with supplies. At least you hope it is.

From the time you take the first 6,000-pound vehicle out

onto the ice to clear away all the snow in early November to the time when the big rigs loaded with 180,000 pounds rumble across in March, the ice is a risk that you have to manage at all times. Dick Robinson knew that. He started his company back in 1968 and it's the biggest trucking and construction outfit in the Northwest Territories. His son Marvin runs it now.

On the morning of Wednesday, December 29, 2004, the ice-building season was in full swing. As many as 150 builders and workers had fanned out across the ice and tundra in Cats, graders, plows, and water trucks. Snow had been cleared or compacted from dozens of bodies of water and layers of ice were added to what Mother Nature already supplied. Helicopters whizzed back and forth in the nosebleed-dry frozen air, strafing the ice below with ground-penetrating radar in search of weak spots that could form with little warning.

It was 50 degrees below zero and Marvin's son Gary was driving a single-axle truck with a snowplow across Prosperous Lake. Running machinery on a lake that is still in the early stages of ice road preparation is dangerous, but Gary was already a fairly experienced driver, having grown up around the ice roads. Still, at twenty-three he wasn't much more than a kid. I was pretty cocksure at his age, I can tell you. Full of piss and vinegar. I know I took a lot of chances.

When a truck drives over a road made of ice, the ice bends to form a bowl around the vehicle and everything underneath gets displaced. As the vehicle moves across the ice, the bowl moves with it. All water that's displaced creates energy waves. The faster you go, the bigger the wave. We call that "pushing your wave." If you're going 30 miles an hour, your wave is going that fast too, but the truck's weight and speed will feed the wave and make it more powerful. If there's a weak spot in the ice, a big wave traveling 30 miles an hour will bust it wide open with tremendous force, like a volcanic eruption. That's why watching your speed is critical. If you have a northbound and a southbound truck coming at each other, both will be pushing waves from opposite directions. Their waves will collide before the trucks pass and you're in big trouble.

Ice that's bending the way it should and handling the weight of the truck and the water it's displacing will crack and pop. That's healthy. I drive with my window open not only to stay alert on a long haul but also to hear the ice cracking out in front of me. If Gary had his window open, he might have heard a deep rumble coming from just in front of his truck. He might have also heard a thunder crack. Those would have been his only warnings.

When Gary approached the oncoming truck, their waves smashed into each other. The ice beneath Gary's truck shot up like a geyser, and down he went. Everything that happened next came at lightning speed. Within seconds, Gary's vehicle—a single-axle truck with a snowplow on the side—was heading for the bottom of the lake. The plow pulled it right down despite pockets of air around the tires and inside the cab. Arctic water, which feels like fire pouring over your body, raced in from the doors and engine compartment. Gary wouldn't have had time to brace himself. The shock to his system would have been too massive. Swallowing water would have felt like swallowing hell's fire. His lungs would have collapsed. The pain would have been unimaginable.

If the truck was dropping at roughly one foot per second, that would be nearly 44 miles an hour. That would have given Gary just thirty seconds to escape the vehicle if it was headed to a bottom any deeper than 30 feet. At those temperatures, swimming that distance would be close to impossible, especially if Gary was injured.

A body reacts to plunging into frigid water by going into cold shock. Cardiac arrest is a serious danger. Gary would have been hyperventilating as soon as the water touched his skin. His blood pressure and pulse would have redlined even as his veins constricted. Back in 2001, Guy Armstrong broke through the ice on Dome Lake and went underwater as his vehicle sank 46 feet to the bottom. He managed to resurface quickly and was rescued from the icy water within thirty seconds, but the shock stopped his heart. All attempts to revive Armstrong failed. He was thirty-seven.

Gary Robinson was young and fit, so his chances would have been a little better. It's easy to panic in this kind of predicament, but Gary had experience, and experience means time. Unless the truck was upside down, there would be a pocket of air at the highest point in the cabin up by the roof. Gary might have tilted his head back and focused first on keeping his airways clear of water. He might have tried to control his breathing. The surrounding water pressure would have made it impossible to open the door, so he would have had to open the window. Electronic windows and power door locks don't function once they're exposed to water, so Gary would have had to smash the window with anything he had handy, like a wrench, or kick it out with his boot. He wouldn't have had to fumble around to get out of his seat, though; by law, ice drivers aren't allowed to wear seat belts—just in case their rig crashes through the ice and they have to jump clear. Of course, without a belt, the force of impact would have slammed him into his windshield.

If the water outside the truck was shallow, Gary would have had about three minutes to escape from his truck, make his way to the surface, then find a solid edge of ice to hoist his body out of the water. But he would have been disoriented when he exited the truck. With precious seconds ticking away, he would have had to remember to follow his air bubbles to the top. Every square inch of his body would have been surrounded by frigid water, but panicking would have used up what little oxygen he had in his lungs. Even if by some miracle he found an air pocket inside the cab big enough to sustain him for several minutes, he still would have had to locate the hole where he went in when he finally made his way up. That would have been tricky on a gray day with low visibility in the water. Worse, at 50 below zero, breached ice starts re-forming immediately, so if Gary was trapped under the new sheet now covering the hole, he'd be in more trouble. Even ice that's only one inch thick can be tough to break through without leverage.

Freezing is dangerous. So is thawing someone out, because you have to be careful not to warm them up too fast. Body core temperature drops to as low as 70 degrees. Blood thickens to the consistency of motor oil. Body organs that were the last to freeze and are the most syrupy will thaw out first, so that the heart can start pumping blood before the extremities thaw. Basically, you have to thaw from the inside out so that the most vital parts suffer the least amount of oxygen deprivation. In the struggle to survive, fingers, toes, ears, and nose are all expendable.

Prosperous Lake is nearly 300 feet deep at the spot where Gary fell in. With his truck plummeting like a dropped anchor, there would be little hope of escaping the vehicle to the top. Gary's skin would have begun to freeze as soon as he had contact with the water. Water inside his body would have transformed into ice crystals that would rip and tear into the surrounding tissue, causing excruciating pain. That pain would pass once his extremities—fingers, toes, ears, and nose—lost sensation. Within a matter of a precious few minutes, hypothermia would have set in. Gary would have felt numb, confused, and very, very sleepy. If he hadn't drowned by then, he would have struggled less and less. He might have noticed that his muscles weren't working right. He would have turned pale, waxy, and blue, especially around the lips. His core body temperature would have crashed and a kind of dementia would have set in. Then he would have slipped into a coma. After five minutes, just about all hope would be gone. Within about twenty minutes, Gary would be well on his way to being frozen solid. That's a terrible way to die, especially when you're only twenty-three.

When I first started working on the ice roads, the other drivers told me that if the ice broke and I had enough advance warning, I should try to jump clear; however, if the truck went down and I was still inside, I should stay inside. "When you go into the water, it's over," they said. "At least if you stay inside, there's a much better chance that the truck company will find your body to send back to your family for burial." In Gary's case, Yellowknife Fire Department divers had trouble finding either the wreck or the driver, so salvage divers with special equipment had to be called in. They brought in a Deepwater ROV system (basically a robotic camera that can operate by remote control even in the harshest conditions) to find the body. The ROV operator said it took him "two weeks of soul-searching and serious drinking to recover."

Gary Robinson had lived around snow, ice, and trucks his whole life. I remember seeing him playing in the RTL shop when he was just a little tyke. He was a good kid. Gary loved camping, fishing, and hunting. He was an avid snowboarder, too. Like many who were born in the Arctic, Gary prided himself on his self-sufficiency. He always carried emergency rescue equipment and was known to have come to the aid of others in need. Losing him in this way, well, that was hard to take. Something like this really shakes up everybody who works out on the ice roads. News of the accident blows right through the radios even before the help gets there. We mourned Gary, but we had loads to carry. It was time to go back to work. Barricades with eerie flashing lights were put down around the hole in the ice where the truck went through. There was no better warning than that for the other truckers to keep their speed down and drive carefully.

On an eighteen-hour run, you have a lot of time to think about a tragedy like this—how it happened, how it might have been prevented. You think about Gary's father, Marvin, and how he once said, "For anybody who's actually working in this business and traveling on the ice, there really isn't a question of *if* you're going to fall in but *when*." But by the end of your first week, after you've logged a hundred hours behind the wheel, it's easy to forget about the risks.

Human nature, I guess.

2.

ON TOP OF
THE WORLD

he Arctic Circle sits like a crown on top of the world, floating with the earth's axial tilt and the pull of the moon. On clear nights, the Big and Little Bear constellations can always be seen overhead. That's where the Arctic name comes from, *Arktos*, the Greek word for "bear." The Arctic is half the size of the United States, but home to only forty thousand hardy souls. That's less than one person for every 10 square miles. In the summer, during the solstice, the sun creeps above the horizon and stays there for twenty-four hours, the period known as "the midnight sun." In the dead of winter, there's twenty-four hours of darkness.

You've never experienced winter until you've lived through one in the far north. It starts in October and doesn't let up until mid-April. With only a few hours of sunlight each day, the nights and the cold can be relentless. With so many hours spent indoors, it can be hard to stay busy and keep your mind active. There are only so many hobbies you can take up or games of hockey or soccer in the snow you can play. Overeating and weight gain, binge drinking and alcoholism, irritability, depression, and other signs of cabin fever are common. The temperatures drop to −70, with winds blowing 60 miles an hour. At that temperature, you throw a pot of boiling water or coffee into the air and it will instantly vaporize and turn into snow. It's cold as hell, but it's also full of riches: silver, gold, uranium, diamonds, and oil, worth tens of billions of dollars. Locating these treasures in the frozen tundra is the easy part. Getting them out of the ground and bringing them from the frozen wasteland to civilization is a lot tougher. That's my job.

For only two months of the year, lakes, ponds, and even parts of the Arctic Ocean itself freeze just enough to create the floating roads that bob and flex over the icy water. During that tiny window of opportunity, ice road truckers brave the earth's fiercest environment in order to haul vital supplies to diamond mines that burrow into the guts of ancient volcanoes, or deliver heavy machinery to oil and natural gas fields in the most remote regions on the planet. Battle-tested Arctic veterans mix it up with the latest crop of wet-behind-the-ears rookies to become the region's lifeline. We put up with the constant thrash of the elements for a chance to earn as much as $70,000 in just over two months.

When December comes, I start getting anxious to get up to the ice roads. Part of it is seeing these people I've known for so long. I figure I can make a go of it just about anyplace on earth, but my heart is in the North and always will be. If I had my way, we would live there, but my wife, Dianne, can't tolerate the extreme cold.

When I'm not on the ice roads, I'm home in Winfield, just outside of Kelowna in British Columbia, 250 miles northeast of Vancouver. Kelowna gets its name from the Indian word for "grizzly bear," which is something I hunt when I get the chance. I built the home we live in, which sits up on a mountain above Okanagan Lake. The lake is as deep as 2,000 feet in places and some people believe that it's the home of Ogopogo, Canada's version of the Loch Ness Monster. I don't know about that. But Kelowna sure is some beautiful country. All around we've got orchards, vineyards, bald eagles, and cougars. I have my own excavation business, and that's the work I do when I'm not on the ice roads. I'd rather be in Yellowknife, but I figure any place that's good enough for Ogopogo is just fine with me.

Whenever I go to Yellowknife, right away I'm back in my element. But before I head north, all my trucks get checked and rechecked. I clean them up inside and out. Sometimes they get a coat of paint to look like new. They all must pass ice road certifications to prove their roadworthiness and extreme climate readiness. Steering, brakes, tires, fuel, and oil lines all must be in tip-top shape. After that, my wife, Dianne, and I go see the kids for Christmas and get away to someplace warm. When I get back, my trucks get one final check. After that, it's time to pack, say good-bye, throttle up, and hit the road. I drive the 1,900 miles from my home in Kelowna, up to

Yellowknife. Sounds like a big adventure to some people, but to me it's just the way I earn my living. To me, it's just business.

Yellowknife is the gateway to the Arctic. Poised at the top of the Northwest Territories, this frontier town serves as a staging area to the longest and most developed ice roads in the world. I first arrived here in the '70s. Right away, the place made a big impression on me. Located on the "Rock" on the north shore of Great Slave Lake, the town was a place of hard living with more than its share of booms and busts—that is, until they discovered gold there in the 1940s. Pretty quick, there were those who came to mine the gold, and then right along after, those who came to mine the miners. Namely, gamblers and prostitutes. Yellowknife was a rough old place back then. Prospectors, Eskimos, and Indians were all living together, and not always peacefully. A bit of that higgledy-piggledy spirit hangs around even today. One of the main streets was named "Ragged Ass Road," the same road Tom Cochrane made famous in his album of the same name. Once known as "Privy Road" because rows of outhouses were the predominant feature, Ragged Ass Road acquired its new name from prospectors who toiled for a year without profit and became "ragged ass poor." The City of Yellowknife later officially adopted the name, which should tell you a thing or two about the local philosophy. Ragged Ass Road is still there down in the Old Town. These days the street sign is welded to its pole to discourage all the people who want to hang it in their homes.

When the ice roads officially open at the end of January, everyone in the truck yard whoops and hollers and blows their air horns. I'm amped to grab that first load and get at her. But rushing is dangerous. Some drivers cheat the speed limit, which is really playing with fire. Others are in such a hurry to get started that they don't tie down their loads properly. That will bite you in the ass down the road, when things start bouncing around. I take my time and do it right. No sense in having to stop on the side of the road to secure a wobbly load.

Slithering east out of Yellowknife is Highway 4, better known as the Ingraham Trail. The road is named in honor of Vic Ingraham, who was a textbook example of a fortune seeker in the early half of the twentieth century. Old Vic was an American born in 1896 who ran north to the whistle call of gold. In 1933, he and three other men were on a tugboat transporting a barge full of supplies to Port Radium on Great Bear Lake when they hit a gale at a time when the barge was dangerously low on fuel.

Great Bear Lake is 190 miles long and 110 miles at the widest spot. When the wind starts howling and the waves smash you about, you might as well be out to sea. The four men were desperately trying to refuel their boat during the worst of the storm. Gasoline sloshed everywhere and when it came into contact with a red-hot exhaust pipe, the tug erupted in flames. Ingraham was on deck at the time and could have easily escaped in the rubber life raft; however, he fought his way through black smoke and fire to the engine room, where two crewmen were trapped. Sadly, despite his heroic efforts, Ingraham couldn't get to the men in time. In fact, he barely made it back to the life raft, where the surviving mate of the tug was waiting. With his hands and feet severely burned, Ingraham climbed into a raft designed to carry only one man. For two days he and the mate drifted in an icy storm before landing on shore. Ingraham lost both of his legs and several fingers on both hands. He soon learned to get around on the crude artificial legs of the time without the use of a cane and earned the nickname "Old Cedar Foot."

Ingraham turned from prospector to prosperous trader and bootlegger to Yellowknife's first hotelier. For a couple of decades the creak of his wooden limbs became one of the most recognizable sounds in Yellowknife. The accident didn't embitter Ingraham. If anything, it solidified who he was. He drank with bush pilots, celebrated with lucky prospectors, but was a soft touch for a hard-luck story. He grub-staked (that is to say, advanced supplies and funds) to any down-and-outers who came his way.

The area outside of Yellowknife was still mainly wilderness at this time. A lot of people had big plans for the area, and the politicians of the 1950s were no exception. Conservative John Diefenbaker—Dief the Chief—campaigned on a promise to open up the Northwest with "Roads to Resources" and was elected prime minister in 1957. As part of this promise, construction began in 1960 on a land route from Yellowknife to Fort Reliance, at the far end of Great Slave Lake. Highway 4, as it was to be called, would create a loop several hundred miles long around Great Slave Lake and would be funded by mineral discoveries along the route. Unfortunately, it soon became apparent that the early projections proved wildly optimistic, and just as quickly as it was started, the "Road to Resources" project was abandoned. The Ingraham Trail now ends at Tibbitt Lake, just 44 miles out of Yellowknife. The Ingraham is a treacherous snake of a narrow, winding road with a mine field of wind shears, sharp shoulders, and a surface that often glazes over with a thin layer of slick ice that's impossible to see. If a driver isn't careful, he can roll his rig even before he makes it onto the ice road. Naming such a road after someone so prominent in local lore might seem a bit strange, but to Yellowknifers it feels about right.

I call the Ingraham the "Ignorant Trail," because it's where dozens of rookie drivers learn what they're getting into. Most are from down south and have never done any driving that didn't involve easy highways and smooth pavement. These newbies go too fast and take the turns too hard. When they go down, they block the other trucks for miles. Time is money out on the ice roads, and you don't get paid for loads that you don't deliver. Every time an ignorant greenhorn spins out, that's money out of my pocket.

I drive a 1999 International known by everyone as the Crow's Nest. When it was new, everybody called it "the condo," because it had the biggest sleeper cabin. My Crow's Nest is a 1998 International 9400 Eagle with a 550 CAT HP N-14 Cummins, 18 Speed Overdrive Transmission, and 44's for the rear end. It's metallic maroon on the outside. The interior is maroon and gray. There's no fancy chrome or decorations and I wouldn't be caught dead with fuzzy dice, but there is plenty of space, enough room for a fridge and a little table. I hang an air freshener to keep the captain's chair from getting too ripe, but this is a space designed for work. The most notable feature is my GPS, which can save your bacon in a storm. But again, no fuzzy dice.

Over the years, I drove so many old trucks for other guys that were little boxes you could hardly move around in. You never really get to sleep. You would just drive until you got tired, then put your feet on your cooler and flop your head down in the back and stay there until you woke up. Then you would sit up and start driving again. It was nice when I got those big condos up there. When my company grew and I started buying trucks for others to drive, I bought big sleepers, because I knew the guys would be happy in them. I also made sure there was plenty of room for provisions. You never know when you're going to be stranded and forced to wait out a bad storm. I bring crates full of food and plan for the worst. If anybody starves to death out there, that's just bad planning.

Just out of town, I cross the Yellowknife River Bridge, come off the Ignorant Trail, slowing down to 5 miles an hour. Some bodies of water on the long hauls are huge and take hours to cross, but Tibbitt Lake is just a taste of the action to come, something to help you break that first sweat and get you on your way. For the next 2 miles on Tibbitt Lake we'll go over open water with just 16 inches of ice standing between us and the bottom of the lake. You're so excited and the adrenaline is pumping. You hear every sound and feel every bump. You're excited to be there and the ice pops and cracks like it's just as excited to have you on board. It's the meeting of two old friends who are both talking and shouting at once.

"You again, you old son of a bitch? Thought you'd learned your lesson."

"Nah, I'm older but no wiser! How the hell are you? Let's see if we can spark the fireworks in that thing you call a brain!"

Once safely across, we'll travel into the Meadows, the first of many rough patches of land between the bodies of water that have been beaten down into portages.

A haul to the farthest diamond mines, Ekati or Tahera, 360 miles away, will require a nerve-jangling trip over the ice roads for more than two days. Eighty-five percent of that run is over water. These are vast lakes and rivers connected by little land bridges of mainly swamplike muskeg that would be passable only by boat or airboat any other time but winter. The lives of those who get our shipments, as well as billions of dollars in commerce for companies such as diamond giant De Beers, are at stake. We haul as much as we can before the ice softens and the chance of crashing through becomes too great.

I love being out on the ice. It gets my blood pumping. I feel alive. It's the last frontier in North America. My wife calls me an adrenaline junkie, but the action and danger fuel me. I came up here decades ago to make my fortune and I guess, in a way, I have. If you're willing to work hard and pay your dues, you can get ahead here, make something of yourself. A man who is willing to work for a little more than sixty days can put a year's worth of wages in his jeans. At the end of an ice road season, he can walk off the ice and buy himself a rig or a business or a house the very next day. When I'm driving, I spend almost as much time planning how I'm going to invest my money as I do driving. It's always on my mind. The money is always right out in front of me on those roads. And of course my family.

I've been married for thirty years. Dianne and I met at a party. She was and is a real looker, but she turned me down flat the first two times I asked her out. Dianne was a shy good girl and I was already a lifetime member of the wild-boy club. I don't usually take no for an answer, so I figured I'd give her one more chance. Third time was the charm.

Dianne and I went out for about a year and a half and then she turned the tables on me and asked me to marry her. Yeah, *she* asked *me*!

"Sure," I said. But I was thinking more like "Sure, someday that would be nice."

At first Dianne told me the date was set for a year and a half away, which seemed like a long way off, but every time I came back from the road I discovered the date had moved up six months. Finally, she told me that our wedding day was only a few months off. I said, "Damn, woman!"

We married young and together raised three children. The girls are all grown up now. Karly is twenty-eight, Chandra-Jo is twenty-six, and Candace is twenty-three. That's right—all girls. Just as I was the only boy growing up in a house full of girls, I became the only man in a house full of growing girls. Wherever I've worked I always came home to a big group of females and I've always been outgunned.

Story of my life.

Dianne's father was a road builder for more than sixty years, and he taught me the ropes. In the early days of our marriage, Dianne used to joke that I spent more time with her dad than with her. Road building is a tough life and you're gone from home for weeks and months at a time. Dianne grew up on a farm just like I did, and she was raised mainly by her mother, who also managed the farm. My being away for three months was actually an improvement from what Dianne was used to. We always timed it so that I would be there for the births of our children, but I missed eleven of Dianne's birthdays in a row because I was on the ice. (It would have been a lot more, but I was laid up one season after my knee surgery.)

I learned from my father how *not* to be a dad. I knew the things I didn't like as a kid and made sure I didn't do them. So no matter how long I was away, Dianne and I still managed to get together a lot as a family. We always had a powerboat for going on the lakes. We like snowmobiling, and when the kids were at home we'd go camping. We had our three girls, of course, and they'd each bring a friend, so there would be six kids and us, and usually the dog. We'd camp out in tents and, boy, would we have fun. In the winters, we always used to lease a cabin up at Beaver and Dee Lake up in Fur Valley and the mountains around Kelowna. We'd go up there on weekends to snowmobile and go tobogganing. Great fun.

When I became a father, I figured that if my kids did only half what I did they'd turn out okay. I kept a pretty tight leash, especially with the boys coming around. Dianne says that when the girls started to date I nearly had a heart attack.

Maybe so, but I kept them busy up at the lake where we had a cabin. We had fireworks, hamburgers, boating, fishing, and water skiing. Most kids don't like hanging out with their parents, but ours did.

I taught all of my girls how to hunt and fish. They were pretty good at it too. That is, until the day Dianne took them clothes shopping at the mall. They came out of that mall looking and acting like girls, and that was pretty much the end of the hunting.

Not having the girls at home has been an adjustment (when the last one moved out, I sold the cabin), but Dianne and I have a good time together and really enjoy each other's company. She says I make her laugh. I always have.

Dianne has never been on the ice roads and doesn't intend to ever visit them. She's been to Yellowknife once and that was enough for her. Dianne said she couldn't abide the cold even though it was summer when she visited. I never really talk about what I've been through out on the ice. I always figured that nobody could really understand what it's like to be out there, so why stress her out needlessly? So Dianne had no idea what I did until she watched the television series. When she told me that the show terrified the hell out of her, I told her not to watch it anymore. Simple, eh?

Dianne starts getting anxious in the weeks leading up to when I'm going to leave. I tell her to get on a plane and go visit the kids if she gets lonely. Sometimes she goes, but mainly she reads a lot. Anything that Dean Koontz or Stephen King has ever written—Dianne has read it. To me, that's some pretty strange reading material for a woman who is all alone in a house far from town in the dead of winter, but whatever floats your boat, I guess.

Where we live on top of the mountain there are bears, and mountain lions prowl around from time to time. When I'm away from home I worry more about that kind of thing than how she'll manage without me. Lots of times I've offered to teach Dianne how to shoot a gun, but she refuses. Guns are fine for me but not for her. I guess she figures that if a bear attacks, she'll just scare it off with a chapter of Stephen King.

Dianne works in a vitamin factory where the shift starts at 4:00 a.m. When I come home, it takes a little while for us to get back in sync because I'm used to being by myself, and she's used to being by herself. We have to get back in the program of things that other people take for granted, like cooking supper and planning meals. But we do. We always do.

Usually, I'm the first to drive a load across the ice. It's considered an honor for the vets to hit the ice first. If it's not me, it's probably Alex Debogorski. Alex is a big ol' bastard of Polish descent who is always quick with a joke. He and I have known each other for thirty years and we have a friendly rivalry going. Usually, I take the crown for most loads and total tonnage hauled, but Alex, well, he has eleven kids. I don't know how he keeps track of them all, but that's a hell of a motivation to get up in the morning. I only have three, so I guess he's got me beat there. Alex used to be a bouncer in the bars around Yellowknife. He was always throwing me out of one place or another, first for underage drinking and later for fighting. Back in '92, Alex ran for mayor of Yellowknife. He had posters of himself all over town with a pig tucked under his arm. I don't know what his political platform was except that he had bought a mess of pigs and maybe he thought that running for mayor was the best way to unload them. He's a driver I respect, not like some of the other jokers on the road.

I don't take the responsibility of first load across the ice lightly. The more time you spend around ice, the more you learn about its unpredictable nature. No matter how much you do ahead of time, nothing on earth can prepare you for that first time you go from the solid earth onto the ice. It's a floating pavement with a brutal death waiting just beneath you if you screw up.

The first thing you notice is that ice dips way down under your weight. Your rig causes a depression around the vehicle, which causes that virgin ice to crack and pop like all hell is breaking loose. Many rookie drivers can't take the pressure. One guy clenched the seat so tight that he tore chunks right out of it. I nicknamed him Ricky Raw Ass. I've sent a lot of so-called tough guys onto the plane back home after that first day. If a new driver listens to my advice, I'm a little more sympathetic. If he isn't, I stay clear of him and whatever happens to him out on the ice road, well, that's his baby.

A lot of times, I'll go up with four or five new guys for the first trip just to show them the ropes. I always stress the point to the guys behind me: "Now, this is your first trip. The ice is thin. Watch your turns. Pay attention to the speed limits. Slow down to 5 miles an hour whenever you get on or off the ice." I try to explain to them about the soul-shattering sound of the breaking ice. I tell them, "Right out in front of you, you can see the ice cracking. If you look past that to the edge of your headlight range, you'll see snow and ice popping right up in the air. That first day it will look like your own little ticker-tape parade."

The snow and ice chips pop right off of it, shooting straight up, dancing like popcorn as high as my windshield. During that first week, most drivers are so busy worrying about the ice cracking under their wheels that they miss the popping farther out, which is crucial to monitoring where your vehicle is in relation to your wave. Watching the ice—listening for those pops—is an essential part of monitoring your progress on the road, as is looking for cracks that can suddenly open without warning. Lots of times, other drivers will give you a heads-up about a crack that has formed and you can check to see if it has healed. But you shouldn't count on other drivers to do your safety monitoring for you. It's your skin, not theirs. You also have to keep an eye on your wheels to make sure they're still turning and that the brakes haven't locked up in the cold.

I figure that monitoring the ice is a big part of my job. I always keep an eye out. New drivers with a few weeks and eight or nine loads under their belts will say, "It's boring out there going twenty miles an hour with nothing to look at for hours." What they don't realize is that just as soon as you let down your guard, that's when the shit hits the fan. I always keep an ear out. If I go faster, the wave under the ice stays closer to the truck, and the ice starts popping right in front of me. When you're driving in the dark with the lights on, you see cracks forming in front of you. Thirty-foot spiderwebs shooting in all directions. Sometimes a crack will open wide and then close up like a clam after you pass. Your mind is screaming, "Holy fuck!" No matter how many years you've been driving, it's still something to get used to on that first trip of the season.

I drive with my windows down at least a bit. Always. I need to know if the ice is healthy and working like it should, or if there's a problem. If there's a rumble or a boom, you'll hear it just before the ice breaks. The only thing you can do is jump out of the truck as far as you can and hope for the best. Most of the time the vehicle is only moving at 20 miles an hour, so at least you won't break your legs or back. I figure you'll have half a chance, which is about as good as it gets in the Arctic. Sometimes a trucker will think the ice is giving way and will jump, only to find out that nothing is wrong. This happens to the rookie drivers who haven't learned what all the noises mean. It's funny to see a driver chasing after his truck. Only the most in-shape usually catch them. I've never jumped from my truck because of a false alarm but I understand why they jump the gun. If you haven't hauled on ice before, there are times when the job can be measured in increments of fear. A sudden crunch or boom of settling ice can cause a driver to pop his top.

The thing to understand is that when something does go wrong, you don't get much warning. Guys who put their trucks on cruise control or blast their music or chatter away on the radio are just asking for trouble. The condition of the ice changes depending on what's going on both above and below the surface. Just because a patch of ice was good yesterday doesn't guarantee that it will be the same today.

One time, a reporter from the *New York Post* rode with me. We had both windows down so he could hear the ice. The combination of freezing wind and cracking ice was so loud that it was just too much for him. After just a couple of miles, he shouted, "Jesus Christ! How do you put up with that?" He was ready to get out. Of course, the ice cracks all year long, but the first trip is the worst, because the ice is new.

When they open the road, you're allowed 50,000 pounds, which is about a 20,000-to-25,000-pound load, because truck and trailer together weigh 25,000 pounds. At that time of the season, there would be about 16 inches of ice under you, and away you go. Every few inches of ice added means heavier and heavier loads, but that first week you start nice and easy.

Ice over a lake is a solid on top of a liquid. It stands to reason that if the ice goes down 12 inches under your weight, then it has to crack. Up or down, left or right, the ice needs to crack in order to displace your weight and support you. There's something wrong if it doesn't. Cracks are superficial and don't damage the integrity of the ice. On the other hand, ice that hasn't been driven on will have air pockets and variations in thickness that will cause stress points and weak spots. If you try to take too much weight over it or travel too fast, the ice will collapse and break apart.

Ice that cracks actually heals itself. Ice that bobs down and comes back exposes more surface area to the surrounding cold air, which causes it to freeze even more. Meanwhile, below the surface, water is rushing in to fill any air cavities. The more you drive over the ice road, the more you bulk it up by adding water. By March, lanes that have seen heavy traffic can have ice that is 7 feet thick. Fly over open water in June and you can still see bits of road floating around like icebergs.

Most new drivers don't appreciate what the Arctic is really like. How could they? They don't realize the force of the snowstorms or the expanse of all the whiteouts. It's a whole package up there, and a lot of people just can't believe it until they're living it. The tree line ends about 100 miles north of Yellowknife, and once you get past that, it's just open tundra. The wind comes up at 60 miles an hour, and if you don't watch out, it will blow you right off the road, especially with those early light loads. You have to be careful when you stop, too. If you open your door with the wind, it can get yanked right out of your hand and get bent or damaged. Now you're out there, 100 miles from anything, with a door that won't close properly. That's trouble for sure. So you learn to open your door with the wind pushing against it. You learn that at times you have to angle your truck just to open the door.

Sometimes you can't see anything out your window. It's snowing and blowing and you have to look for snowbanks and hope that you're still on the road. Other times, you have visibility for miles and miles but there's nothing to see but white, flat tundra. On a sunny day, you look out as far as the eye can see and it looks like a white ocean, a vast wide-open space of nothing but white. If you don't wear polarized glasses you'll go snow-blind. All that white and open space spooks some drivers.

And then there's the cold. The cold stings your face and freezes your nostrils so you can't breathe. Hands freeze and turn into stiff claws. The wind rips at your clothes. It might snatch your hat so fast that you never see it again, or fling the glasses right off your face. Everything hitting you at once scares the shit out of the new drivers. They're terrified, thinking they're about to die. On top of it, you're asking them to do a job and perform a duty.

One of my drivers, Rick Yemm, was gung-ho his first year. Rick is a hardworking guy who has always done a good job for me down in Kelowna, where I live during the year. He's not especially big or tough, but he'll do whatever you tell him to and keep at her until he gets the project done. He's a stepdad to his wife's handicapped kid and, like me, never had much of a home life growing up. I met Rick at a bowling alley and we started to bowl together. He was just a kid at the time and I got him his first job driving a rock truck. He had never been around heavy machinery before so I taught him everything and he just went on from there. He's been like my little brother for seventeen years. He will give his last dime to a friend in need. The only thing is: you have to keep straightening him out. Still, when Rick said he wanted to take on the ice roads, I said, "Let's give it a shot."

Right out of the gate, Rick thought it would be funny to play the cocky rookie.

"Yeah, I'm going to crush you, Hugh," he said.

The ice road has its share of tough guys and one-trip cowboys and has dealt with them accordingly. I told him as much.

"Talk is cheap," I said. "Whiskey costs money, buddy. Wait until you get your ass up there."

Unfortunately, I didn't get to take Rick on his first trip.

Drivers are given very specific departure schedules, called tee times, so that they don't all rush out onto the ice at the same time. I had seven guys with me on my tee time, but Rick wasn't one of them. He went up with somebody else and nobody cared to show him the ropes. That first time out from Tibbitt, Rick was sick to his stomach. By the time he was on his fourth trip, his eyes were getting black with circles. He was sicker than a dog. I figured he'd get the hang of it, but then my buddy Reggie said, "You better talk to Rick. He's going to have a nervous breakdown."

Ol' Reg Lanfrancois is one of my best friends out there on the road. Reg was a hard-rock miner from back East in Ontario who came to Yellowknife in '91 looking to mine gold. He found the ice roads instead. Reg is a big boy, about the same size as me, but a little bigger around the middle. I call him "Gooey." People are always asking me why I call him that, but I figure it's none of their business so I never told them. However, the third part of my Three Rules for Partying credo (never turn down a free beer, don't waste a hard-on, and don't trust the fart) comes from my good buddy Reg. You know that somebody who can come up with that is worth hanging around with. Most of the time, that is. In the middle of one of our seasons, Reg had picked up some sort of intestinal trouble and a bad case of diarrhea that wouldn't let up. Believe me, you don't want to be out on the ice one hundred miles from a toilet when you have the shits. Picking up a nickname is the least of your worries.

But Reg is a good guy. When the season is over and I haven't seen him for nine months at a time I can still call him up from anywhere in the world and say, "Hey, Gooey! How's it goin'?" and Reg will roar with laughter. He knows exactly who's on the other end of the line. I kid Reg that he's one of the few good Frenchmen I know. I also bug him about his English, about the way he always says "nort'" instead of "north." Things like that.

"For chrissakes," I'll say, "you've been coming up here for twenty years now, when are you going to learn how to speak English?"

Reg tells me to fuck off. I'm the only one that can get away with teasing him about his accent, and the only one who can call him Gooey. For his part, he's about the only one who can tell me where to go every time I see him.

I'm glad Reg is in my corner. He knows the ice as well as I do. He doesn't hesitate to wade into a tough situation, so he's the one you want to have with you if the odds are one-sided. So when Reg told me that Rick was struggling, I paid attention.

I caught up with Rick in the truck yard.

"Reg says you're having a problem," I said. "What's up?"

At first he denied it, but he eventually came clean. "I don't know if I can take this. I'm terrified."

Rick was on the edge. When I'm in a tough situation, I look at it like it's a challenge or an adventure, but Rick let his nerves get to him.

"Get a load," I said. "You're coming with me."

Over the next several days, I coached Rick on how to drive on the ice roads and what to listen for. I talked to him nonstop over the radio for hours, taking him through every portage and onto every lake.

"How you making her?" I'd ask.

"Doing real good, Hugh," he'd say.

"Watch out for this turn coming up. She's a tricky son of a bitch."

"Aye-aye, Captain!" Rick would say.

We delivered his load and I said, "Well, you made it up here loaded, so going back is nothing. Just do the speed limit you're doing and everything will be fine." I made one more trip with him, just to be sure, and after that, Rick was set. I was proud of him for sticking it out and making it through. He still ended up getting homesick and left before the season was done. He came back the next year, cowboying it up for the TV cameras and abusing the trucks. He ended up quitting again. I did my best to make a driver out of him, and he came close. In the end, the ice roads weren't for him.

Rick may have played the fool for the cameras but he's still a gamer in his own way and still my friend so I don't like people running him down. Last year, I was signing autographs at a NASCAR event when a guy came up and said he was pleased to meet me. We were shaking hands when he said, "If Rick were here, I'd knock his block off."

Instead of letting go of his hand, I grabbed it tight and pulled him in close.

"If Rick were here, he'd take your head right off your shoulders." He was a pretty big guy and Rick isn't much of a fighter, but all the same. It's crazy how worked up people get.

Those cameras sure changed a lot of things, I don't mind telling you. Those of us who drive the ice roads are pretty much used to just getting on with it—doing our job, keeping our noses to the grindstone and our tires on the ice. Sure, there'd be beers and brawls and that sort of thing, but nobody knew who we were and what we were doing. And we liked it that way. When the television reality series *Ice Road Truckers* (IRT) came along, suddenly we were blasted onto television screens around the world. Kind of unbelievable.

Back in 2007, the *Ice Road Truckers* premiere was seen by 3.4 million viewers in the United States, where it became the most-watched original telecast in the History Channel's twelve-year history. Since then, the show has now been seen all around the world throughout North America, Europe, Africa, the United Kingdom, Australia, and New Zealand. Alex Debogorski and I have been main "characters" on the show from the beginning. I'm told that just in the United States alone, more than 3 million viewers tune in to watch us each week. That's quite an audience, but not something I concern myself with. Mainly, I go about my business and don't think about the cameras following me around, which isn't always easy.

Producer Dolores Gavin had the original idea of doing a show about us. In March of 2006, producer Thom Beers and some of his crew showed up in Yellowknife all the way from Los Angeles. That would be Hollywood, I guess. They were asking a lot of questions about the ice roads and stopped by Tli Cho Trucking looking to put cameras in trucks. They were told, "You should talk to Hugh Rowland. He's been running the roads longer than just about anybody. Hugh has a small fleet and is quite a character."

I was charging hard to close out the 2006 season and

didn't run into the Hollywood guys. I didn't hear about them, and no one at Tli Cho mentioned it either. However, a few weeks later, they called me at my home in Kelowna and said they wanted to shoot some footage of me on the ice roads.

"The winter road is done for the year. You have to talk to me next November or December," I said bluntly.

That was the extent of the conversation. I was pretty sure that someone was trying to pull my leg, so I was surprised when they followed up in November of 2006. Thom said, "Hello, Hugh, we spoke with you about six months ago about putting some cameras in your trucks?"

I had completely forgotten about the previous conversation.

"You weren't very receptive at the time, but we thought we'd try again."

"What is this about, then?"

Thom told me they wanted to do a little documentary on the ice road truckers. I remember seeing a CBC (Canadian Broadcasting Company) documentary about John Denison, the father of the ice roads. His story was well known by most people in the Northwest Territories but seldom told outside of the area. I knew the story was important, and I was proud of my connection to his world. So I listened to Thom's pitch a little more and then I said, "What the hell . . . I'll do it—"

He started to thank me and I cut him off.

"Just tell your people to stay out of the way of my work and the work of my drivers, because the second somebody starts to cost me money, I'll throw the camera out of a moving truck. And if there's a cameraman attached to the camera, I'll throw him out too."

Thom gave me his assurance that the cameras would stay out of the way.

I kind of surprised myself by agreeing to the situation. There was no money involved and, at first, I couldn't figure out why I had done it. I guess I figured that this was a way to put the spotlight on the Territories and what we're all doing there. The people there have endured and suffered for so long. I relate to that especially, because for a long time their struggles have been my struggles. So I said, "Okay."

I'm very proud to see that their story has been brought to people all over the world. In that sense, I'm grateful to the show.

Next to mine, Alex Debogorski's mug is the most recognizable on *Ice Road Truckers*. Yeah, I know. Neither of us is very pretty. Alex has been an ice road warrior for about as long as I have. He's a good guy and I respect him the way you do when you've been through stuff with somebody. And we've been through a lot—on the roads and off. Just about a year ago, for example, in 2008, we were in the middle of our season up in Inuvik when Alex told me he was experiencing shortness of breath. Viagra can cure most of the things that Alex usually complains about, but this—well, this was different. Shortness of breath? That's major. And there was more. Alex was coughing blood.

"Don't mess around with something like that," I told him. "Get to the doctor right away."

Me and doctors, well, I'll put off going as long as I can,

but you don't mess around with something like this, especially when you're getting behind the wheel. But Alex being Alex, he decided he would tough it out and worry about it when the season ended four weeks later. He saddled up and went onto the ice with a forty-ton, four-story-high section of drilling rig substructure for the natural gas platform at Langley. He seemed to be doing okay for a time, but in his weakened state, Alex missed a turn and was off course for nine hours.

When I heard that Alex went off the road I knew that something was really wrong. He never would have done something like that if he were feeling okay.

Alex looked like hell warmed over when he finally arrived at Langley. His heart was racing and his face was pale. Management quickly sidelined him and sent him to the ER. Alex had an embolism in the past and has a history of heart problems. He even had open-heart surgery a few years ago. Now a blood clot had formed in his lungs. A blood clot. Wow. That sure is some major shit. A blood clot can lead to a heart attack or a stroke and there isn't any amount of Viagra in the world that's going to help you with that. Had he continued driving for another day, Alex might have cashed it in and we would have lost him. Instead, he was medevac airlifted 1,000 miles to a state-of-the-art hospital in Yellowknife. They caught the clot in time, but Alex's ice road season was finished.

You know, Alex said once that "everybody should get up in the morning and say a prayer, you know, for the day, for protection and guidance, and to give thanks for this day."

I'm not a religious guy, but I say Amen to that.

There's an old saying that the two happiest days of a boat owner's life are the day he buys the boat and the day he sells the boat. That's a little like how I feel about the *IRT* nowadays. I remember in the first season, when I heard that three of my trucks were parked in the Meadows at the start of the ice road for some sort of shoot, I nearly lost it. I drove over there and threw the cameras out of the truck and told them not to come back. Keep in mind that I was doing this for free, which means that I was losing my income for a good part of the season. The producers responded quickly with compensation as well as guidelines that they haven't always been able to stick to. Sometimes someone would come to me and say, "We missed that shot. Would you mind backing it up and doing it again?" I would shoot them the shaft and tell them to get out of my way.

"You know better than that. I don't do bullshit," I'll say. "Right now, you are costing me money."

I've never had trouble with my drivers, but that first season, guys like Rick went to hell on me. My drivers had always stayed clear of the bars, but now they were being egged on to act like drunken cowboys who would call me with grievances, real or imagined. I guess it made for good drama, but I didn't like it. It was a good thing that the show moved on to Inuvik and Alaska, where I was a hired gun and didn't have a crew. Otherwise, I might have murdered one of my drivers.

I think that *Ice Road Truckers* gives a good sense of the risks of being an ice road driver, but it also created conflicts among the drivers. I guess that the nature of television is to make us into caricatures of who we really are, so I became the egotistical, foul-mouthed son of a bitch. That's good entertainment but it wasn't very realistic. I certainly wouldn't get hired to drive year after year if that was my attitude.

All that said, I think we put most so-called reality shows to shame. People like the true-life adventure at its no-nonsense best. I think *IRT* delivers that. In a world that sometimes seems all topsy-turvy, we work hard to get the job done. Viewers from all over the world contact me saying that they appreciate that. When you hear from some stranger who has lost a livelihood or job but is writing to say they are worried about us, well, it just hits home.

3

DOGS AND CATS

efore there were ice roads or even roads in the Northwest Territory, there were dogsleds. For hundreds of years, dogs were used by the Indians to guard their reindeer herds, haul food, and carry other supplies. When the explorers, trappers, and settlers arrived, dogsleds became a lifeline—the main form of winter transportation and the best way to haul cargo over land. They transported not only furs but hundreds of pounds of buffalo tongues, dried meat, flour, and cakes, as well as bladders of grease for cooking.

Prior to the nineteenth century, the trails weren't well established; most were no wider than deer runs, which explains why the sleds were so narrow and the teams so small—two or four dogs per team. The sled teams may have been severely limited by what they could carry (mainly ammunition, tobacco, alcohol, and fuel), but the best drivers could brave the fiercest storms and still travel up to 80 miles a day. When the trails were widened, the size of the sleds and the dog teams increased, with the result that the teams could be used to pull the heavy loads that made the Alaskan Gold Rush of 1896 possible. If we ice road truckers of today have a "dash for the cash," then I guess the dogs had the "mush to the rush."

Despite their glorious history, dogsleds had limitations. Freight was limited to a few hundred pounds and, depending on the size of your team, you had a lot of mouths to feed. It wasn't until the 1930s when Cat trains (from the brand name "Caterpillar") appeared in the Northwest. These slow-moving, heavy-equipment convoys weren't designed to travel great distances, but they could haul thousands of pounds and never ate your boots. By the 1950s, quicker vehicles, like trucks, were brought in for hauling, so Cats were confined to clearing and construction duties.

I first drove the Cat owned by my father when I was nine years old, so I've got a soft spot for them. I would plow a road to feed the cows in winter as part of my daily chores. I've always worked at something. Always pulled my weight. And I've done it all, from drilling and blasting to paving roads to sewer and water. I've done a lot of risky and dangerous work, putting my life on the line just to get the job done. I guess you could say I'm a jack-of-all-trades and master of none.

I've been working for the big outfits since I was fifteen. I've always caught on quick. No matter what job I started with, before long, I ended up being the boss. By the time I was sixteen, I was already in charge of guys who were forty. That's just the way I am. When I was sixteen years old and living on my own in Yellowknife I was desperate to work. I stopped by a company with some name like Clark Construction. Everyone was out except for a mechanic. I told him I was eighteen and needed a job.

"Well, what can you run?" he asks.

I looked around the yard and there were Cats and hoes and just about everything else. "I can run anything you've got here." Then I added, "I can run anything you've got here better than anybody who already works for you." That gave him a big laugh.

"All right, you cocky son of a bitch, hold on a minute." The mechanic gets on the radio and calls the owner. "I got a guy here that says he's eighteen, but is going on forty-five," I hear him say.

The voice on the other end of the radio answers back, "Oh, yeah? Well, we need a backhoe operator. Why don't you go for lunch but tell him to dig a trench so you can put that tank in. Tell him to do that, and then you'll talk to him after lunch and see how he makes out."

The machine in question looked like an antique. They were calling my bluff with the biggest pile of rust they had in the yard. Luckily, it just so happened that that machine was the same one that we had back on the farm for digging water lines.

"Sure, I'll do that. No problem."

Twenty minutes later I was standing in front of the mechanic again. He looked up from his mouthful of sandwich.

"Can't get her running?"

"No, it's done."

"It's *done!*" he repeated and laughed. "All right, let's get this over with." The mechanic put down his sandwich and walked outside.

"Holy . . . shit," the mechanic was muttering to himself.

"What?" I asked.

"Well, nobody here could even run that old piece of crap."

We both started laughing.

"Holy shit!" he slapped his side and shouted. The mechanic shook my hand. "Welcome aboard!"

I've always been proud of the way I could tweak a machine to the best of its ability and make it perform better. Whatever it is, I can make it put out that little extra that will get you a little bit more money. As far back as I can remember, I've been good at that. Same goes for people. I can make them work harder and longer than they ever dreamed possible. Everyone makes the most money of their lives when they work with me.

At sixteen, I worked as a Cat skinner, operating a bulldozer in the bush, moving earth to build a road through the wilderness far from town and people. We have a lot of wilderness in Canada, and bulldozers are used to clear the terrain. One day in the early spring, I was building a temporary road or "new cut" road for oil exploration. These are narrow, rugged roads that are only wide enough for one vehicle at a time. I was on a D7, a medium-size track-type bulldozer that weighed about twenty-two tons. D7s were a pretty common workhorse up in the Territories, because you could haul them from location to location without having to dismantle them. Because Caterpillar offers a variety of blades for the D7, it's also a versatile machine. You can push snow, move all kinds of material, and do grade work too. "Grade work" is the first step in building a road. You smooth out a roadbed with earth-moving equipment to create something capable of accommodating a vehicle.

The D7 has been around in one form or another since 1938. It's battle-proven and doesn't break down.

Clearing a temporary road is a one-man job, so I was working alone. I remember that it had warmed up enough to rain all day. A cold rain just kept up, making everything sloppy and miserable. The temperature was dropping quickly, but I didn't really pay any attention, because I had heat coming off the engine. It was time to stretch my legs and take a piss break, so I shut down, climbed out of the seat, and stepped onto the track. The machine was covered in slick mud. That's how I slipped off the Cat. I put my foot down and my leg slammed right through the space between the blade and the track, and that's where I stayed. The ligaments in my leg were all torn to hell. I felt that right away. The pain was excruciating. It was six thirty at night and getting cold. The temperature kept dropping until it was about 40 below zero.

The blade that had me pinned down weighed at least 3,500 pounds. Shit. No way could I budge it with just my hands. But there was an iron bar lying nearby. It wouldn't be enough to wedge under the blade and pull out my leg, but I figured if I could get ahold of it, I could at least reach one of my gloves that I had left up on the Cat. I stretched out for all I was worth, and, at first, the bar was just out of reach. I kept at it, clawing, lunging, and swearing until, finally, I got it. Once I had the bar, I used it to get to a standing position; then I used it again to fish for the glove. The tricky part was getting the bar inside the glove without knocking it to a place I couldn't see or reach. Pain shot through one whole side of my body and the heaviness of the bar caused my arm to shake. The glove kept creeping closer and closer to the edge. A few times I almost lost it, but then—success. I got the glove. Having it would keep my hand from freezing.

I'm not an excitable guy. Even at sixteen, I kept a cool head when I was in a mess. But I was overheated and sweating like a pig after what seemed like an hour but was probably only about fifteen or twenty minutes. Running up your temperature when it's that cold and you're immobile is dangerous, because you run the risk of getting the chills as soon as your body starts cooling down, but I figured I'd be okay. I knew help was coming, that after a section of wilderness was cleared, a low-bed truck would come to move the bulldozer to the next location. I also knew that it probably wasn't likely to come soon. The driver could show up anytime, as long as he got me to the next spot by seven in the morning.

Time passes slowly in that kind of situation. The pain was stabbing up from my knee and shooting straight through my body. I had no way to keep circulation going to that leg, and it was getting cold as hell out there. At first I thought about some of the tight spots I'd been in: car wrecks, thrown from horses and bulls, other times I'd been caught out in the bush in bad weather. It was amazing that I had been through so much and was still alive. I decided this time was no different and that I better keep my wits about me. But the darkness was brutal. The North gets dark like you wouldn't believe. It's not the same as city-dark. It's pitch-black. Until the stars come out, you can't see your hand in front of your face.

This was no time to daydream or nod off. Bears and packs of wolves roamed these woods and I didn't want to be on the menu. I kept the iron bar close by and concentrated on the surrounding forest. I lay there in the frozen mud on my back, listening for sounds of the low-bed approaching or anything prowling in the underbrush. If I heard a branch crack, I'd listen and sometimes give a big yell. Maybe that was a lynx nosing around; it was hard to tell. I happened to have my headgear in my pocket and the one glove on. That turned out to be a pretty good bit of luck. I might have just as soon left the hat and both gloves up on the controls. I could have easily frozen my foot, especially my toes, because of the lack of circulation and the position it was in. Of course, that's just frostbite, but frostbite is bad enough. If you've ever held your hand over a hot fire then pulled it away, if you've ever felt that burning sensation on your skin . . . that's what frostbite is like.

So I was lying there in the frozen mud like an animal in a bear trap, thinking, "Now what the fuck am I going to do?" This was 1978, so there were no cell phones or two-way radios or anything like that. After getting the bar and then the glove, I figured the only other thing I could do was to conserve my energy and wait, so that's what I did. I had the ache in my leg to keep me company. Because of the pain, I tried not to move around too much. I just kept my mind on that low-bed coming. I was only sixteen, but I had already been in all kinds of scrapes in all kinds of weather, so I wasn't worried or scared, just plenty pissed off. I mean, how long was I supposed to lie there in the cold?

Seven hours later, at one thirty in the morning, the driver arrived. He didn't act especially surprised or say much.

"Holy Christ! Looks like you got yourself into one hell of a situation. . . . Well, let's get you out."

He inserted the bar, pried up the blade, and pulled my leg out. I was stiff as a board by then. Somehow I got to my feet. My skull was pounding and I was light-headed. I shook it off. I didn't go to the hospital or anything like that. I had to be at the next location to be cleared, ready to start work at seven in the morning. So I just started up my pickup and followed the driver to the next site. We unloaded the Cat, and I went to work.

I never did get to the doctor. Not that day, not for a long time. I spent the next twenty years living with that bad knee, pretty much my whole adult life, all because I didn't want to miss any workdays. In '98, I slipped on my own excavator, working over on one of the local mountains near my home in Kelowna. I slipped on the track and the knee popped sideways, right out of joint. I had to crawl up the hill, get in my truck, and drive myself over mountain roads to the hospital. There they told me, "You won't walk again unless you have this knee rebuilt. You can't put this off anymore."

So I had reconstructive knee surgery. The surgeon made an incision around the knee, filled it up with air, blew all the meat out around the bone, and then went in there and took the kneecap off. They scraped all the arthritis out, and then they made new ligaments and cartilage with my own hamstrings. They sewed it all back up and that was it. I was laid up for about seven months, hobbling around on crutches. I had to do a hell of a lot of physical exercise with my leg until it was better. The pain was overwhelming at times, but I did the exercises every day.

Far as I'm concerned, the knee is as good as new. That doctor did one hell of a job. I probably should have taken care of it a long time ago, but back then it wasn't anything I even considered. I had started a family with Dianne when I was eighteen, and there was money to be made and work to be done. I learned from an early age that if you weren't working, you weren't making money. Head down, ass up, and carry on. That's my attitude.

I've worked hard since I was a kid, but in my early twenties I learned the endurance necessary for a life on the ice. Before trucking on the ice roads, from 1978 until the mid-'80s, I worked in the oil fields of British Columbia. People had known about the existence of oil since the eighteenth century, when explorers reported seeing riverbanks crusted over with a mixture of tarlike oil and sand. It took about a hundred years for them to figure out what to do with their discovery, so use was confined to a makeshift caulking for boats and canoes in need of emergency repair. When whale oil used for lamps in homes became scarce, in the mid-1800s, trappers and settlers began lighting their homes with what they called "coal gas."

In the 1920s, homesteaders began reporting the presence of oil seeps in the Peace River area. Someone would go to put in a fence post and, just like Jed Clampett, bubbling crude oil would fill in the hole. A seep doesn't always mean a lot of oil; however, because many petroleum discoveries in the world had been made near seeps, there was already interest in British Columbia. In the early 1930s, the BC government placed all of the Peace River lands under reserve to discourage control by American interests. By the start of World War II, strategic oil reserves were established in the "Deep Basin" region of northeastern BC, south of Dawson Creek and adjacent to the Alberta border. Despite all that bureaucratic activity, relatively little actual drilling took place. The land was raw and inaccessible "moose pasture," and only wildcatters had the temerity to get in there. Theirs was a high-risk, high-cost, and low-yield endeavor. They would venture into the unknown, hoping to literally stumble across oil. The area they covered was vast. It was like looking for a needle in a field of needles. And as was always the case in the Northwest, finding something of worth wasn't always an issue—getting it out of the ground and to market was the problem.

By the time I came along in the late '70s, most of those logistical issues had been solved. Political problems in the Middle East resulted in an energy crisis that created a frenzy of activity. Oil companies needed every able-bodied man they could get. That was me.

My job was to cut trees and clear roads for petroleum exploration. I'd go up to Peace River for three months, pretty much working six and seven days a week, which was par for the course. You were expected to put in at least twelve-hour days, and for that you were well compensated. Even back in the late '70s, I could clear anywhere from $10,000 to $16,000 a month. The oil companies paid for everything and even bought me a brand-new company truck. They paid for my food, cigarettes, and clothes. A lot of times I would get paid for a twenty-four-hour workday because I literally stayed on the Cat for a couple of days at a time. We worked in the middle of nowhere, far from anyone or anything. Guys would fly in and out by chopper. There were no roads, so helicopters were the only way you could get to a work site. If the chopper couldn't make it to pick you up, you slept on the Cat. You had a canvas tarp that you put over your head and you went to sleep in your seat, running the engine to keep warm. I learned to sleep sitting up like a cowboy on his horse. If you moved around too much, you would risk falling off your perch and onto the ground. It was a rude way to wake up.

There were all different groups working out there. The one I was with had twelve men and twelve Cats. Twelve men was a pretty typically sized unit. We would be given a project to make a road that went over a mountain. You would start at the bottom, where the brush and trees were so thick you wouldn't see a bear even if it was 15 feet in front of you.

I would put in three stakes in a line, go out in front of them, and then line up dead center, where I would start to cut a line 180 miles straight through the brush, driving the

Cat. Every time I couldn't see the stakes, I'd have a saw man come and set up a new stake for me. I would be on the Cat driving, say, due east, and a guy would be setting the line behind me. I had a topographical map that I followed, which let me know what was up ahead. I knew if I was about to cross a creek or ridge, I would cut for eight hours, then clean my way up for eight hours all the way back. I might put in sixteen or seventeen hours doing that, plus drive two hours there and two hours back. So those were twenty- or twenty-one-hour days. Of course, all of us would do it all over again the next day. But you only had a couple months of doing that before winter would come and shut us down for the season. So I was racing the clock with every shift.

At the other end of my 180 miles, I would pound in a stake that meant that it was the "end of the line." That's where I'd stop. At 180 miles, if I was off by just a single degree, I might figure to be off my line by 500 to 1,000 feet. One year, I came within 14 feet of the line; however, 500 to 1,000 feet was more typical, and considered to be "close enough." After I was done, the company would come in and do seismic testing, and only then would they be able to determine if there was oil in sufficient quantities for commercial development down there. If the result showed promise, they would build a lease road, bring in an oil rig, and start drilling for oil.

We worked in two-man teams. It was always two men: two Cats on every side of the line. You always made the clearing two Cats wide. One Cat would go in, and the other Cat would come behind him. The first Cat would stay far enough ahead so that when you were knocking your trees down, the trees the second Cat was knocking down wouldn't hit the first. If a tree came down on top of you, you'd never hear or see it coming. There was a good chance of being killed.

We put in lots of hours. That was the hardest part of the job. At the end of a couple months, you were played right out because you never got any real sleep. You'd just be sleeping on the Cat, sleeping on the seat with just a bit of thin canvas. The fan was turned back, so the heat off the engine was the only warmth you'd get. It was 40 below out, but you got used to it.

Once I got double pneumonia working out there. I never thought I was going to die, but I never felt like that before, either. I just thought I was sick, but it got worse and worse. I just worked right through it, burning up even though it was 50 below. The water ran off me like I was in a sauna. I'd finally get into the camp and the reverse would happen. I would be in a shower with the water turned as hot as it would go, and I'd be shivering to death. The best thing I could've done would be to go to the doctor, but we might have been 175 miles from anyone. So, again, I never went. Of course, I paid the price, and now my lungs are scarred.

We worked all day and partied and drank hard every night. When I first started doing this work, I was just a kid. You'd go to a Cat camp, and eight guys would share one small bunkhouse that was maybe 10 feet by 10 feet. In that space there were four beds, and two shifts, twenty-four hours a day, twelve hours each. You'd have one cook and one shower. Shifts ran 24/7 because of the short season. So at the completion of a shift, when I'd head back to the camp, the guy who was heading out would get out of my bed and roll up his sleeping bag. Then I'd roll out my sleeping bag and get in the bed.

Of course, with that many men in such close quarters, there's going to be fights. And there were. Every day. A lot of these were dry camps, but every time you had a new guy arrive, or somebody would come in from a day off, he'd sneak out to the nearest town, which might be a couple hundred miles away. Whenever the cook went into town to get groceries, everybody sent money. When the cook came back, out would come the 40-pounders. Forty-pounders were 40 ounces of cheap, hard alcohol, shit like five star whiskey or black-label anything. You'd break out the 40-pounders, and then there'd be a fight that night. The fights usually started because everybody was the best Cat skinner in the world, and everybody could run a Cat better than the next guy. One of us would make a boast, and the next thing you knew, there would be a knock-down, drag-out brawl. But come morning, you'd forget all about it, and you'd all be best friends again.

I was no stranger to fighting. If I didn't start a brawl, I could always end it. My brother-in-law Billy always fought alongside me in the bars. He was just a little guy but he'd always back me up. We cleared out many a bar in Yellowknife. Eventually, the cops would come. We would end up fighting them, too, which would land us in jail overnight. Come morning, when we didn't wander in, my sister Terry would come looking for us. She always knew to head over to the jail.

I never hesitated to mix it up in the oil camps but unlike

some of the other guys, I was always able to answer the bell for work in the morning. I never got fired. I figured that if I worked hard, I could play hard, but I couldn't have one without the other. By fighting, I was mostly blowing off steam because, often, work on the roads was dangerous.

One time, an older guy named Bill and I cut seismic line on the night shift. We were cutting trees—going through pitch-black forest, miles from anywhere. We had just the lights from our Cats to guide us. It was a pretty surreal experience to be crashing your way through the darkness, unable to see anywhere except a few unobstructed feet directly in front of you.

It was just about midnight, and Bill was ahead of me. Now, we always stop to have coffee and something to eat at midnight. I saw Bill up ahead. By that I mean that I saw his lights. So I thought, okay, I'll go up there, and he'll flash his lights at me when I can get close enough to stop for a break.

But by the time I got closer, Bill's lights were gone. I figured he must have been stopped, so I just kept cutting. All of a sudden, there was nothing there. Nothing. I went straight down with the Cat, plunging down a 300-foot cliff. Somehow, I never rolled or went end-over-end. The tracks were off the ground much of the time, sending the Cat and me airborne. By some kind of a miracle, I just went straight down. Finally, I slammed into the bottom of the cliff, where I found Bill's Cat. It had slid sideways right at the cliff bottom. He wasn't on it. Right away, I feared the worst.

I parked right beside Bill's Cat and eased off mine.

I was just about to start a search when I glanced over to

a spot where Bill was calmly drinking a cup of coffee. As I walked over he said, "Well, I was wondering how long it was going to take you to get down here. Going over a cliff like that, I just held on for dear life, and this is where I ended up . . . I just about shit my pants, Hugh. And now here you are right beside me."

"Holy fuck," I said. "If I had known the cliff was there, I would have sunk my ripper in and dug my way down here."

That's what I do to climb down a mountain like that. I just dig the ripper in with a full blade of dirt and down I go. You can go down anything you want that way. Of course, you won't get back up it, but you can go down. Unfortunately, we had no idea there was a steep drop-off. It was midnight and dark.

That incident scared the shit out of both of us, but we were both fine. Even the machines were in working condition. It's a wonder one or both of us didn't get killed. I was only twenty-five. Bill was about fifty-five.

It was good money, but a hard, dirty life.

Dogs and Cats

4

BIG JOHN

f there's one thing that people in the Northwest Territories understand, it's ingenuity. With so little contact with the outside world, they've learned to rely on themselves and on their wits. It's as simple as that. Until recently, people in the NWT were pretty much isolated in the winter, which is why anybody who made their way to that part of the world had to be cut from a different cloth, a different breed altogether. The people who thrive up here have one part the outlaw and one part the "get her done" spirit that, I guess, comes from the many legends that blazed a trail through the rugged Northwest Territories.

Probably the most famous legend was Albert Johnson, aka "The Mad Trapper." Johnson was a legend and sort of a folk hero in those parts, and his story is known all over the world. Following a dispute over traps and, I think, a dog, Johnson shot and killed one Mountie and severely wounded another. This was in 1932, and the circumstances surrounding the event are mysterious and a matter of dispute even today. What is known is that after the shooting, Johnson led the Mounties on a wild and woolly chase through the meanest part of winter in the Arctic wilderness. There was a massive manhunt gunning for him, but Johnson eluded capture for forty-five days, besting blizzards and climbing 7,000-foot mountain passes with nothing more than a rifle and the pack on his back. It took an airplane to find, hunt, and kill him. By then, Johnson was half-starved and weighed 85 pounds but still made a last stand. There are all sorts of rumors about Johnson. They say that he was found with more than $2,000 on his body, not to mention some gold, a compass, some fishhooks, a dead squirrel, and a couple of gold teeth presumed to be his.

My grandpa Hugh knew Johnson well. He said that Johnson was a nice young fella and that they must've done something to set him off. According to Grandpa, Johnson was very much a loner, and he didn't make friends easily. Matter of fact, Grandpa was like that too. He was just a big old burly bastard. Funny thing was, during the whole manhunt no one ever heard Johnson say a word. Not one. When Yellowknifers tell the story, they always say that part with pride and respect.

Yellowknifers are self-sufficient and strong, with one hell of an independent streak. They've got to be; otherwise, they won't make it. It can be a tough life, up North. Prior to the 1950s, people in the NWT brought goods in by boat or plane in the summer and by dog teams pulling freight sleds or the occasional Cat train in the winter.

Big John

55

Planes required brash bush pilots like Max Ward and Willy Laserich, two legendary daredevils of the North who could fly into the many uncharted areas of the Arctic and land on wheels, skis, or floats. Because airports were few and far between, refueling consisted of either setting up private fuel stations or burying and then relocating fuel dumps—no easy feat in the middle of the vast wilderness. Laserich was especially famous for carrying barrels and barrels of fuel, which would essentially transform his DC-4 four-engine prop airplane into a flying bomb. The DC-4 was capable of carrying 20,000 pounds of cargo, so that was one big bomb.

Laserich kept getting turned down for a commercial license, but that didn't stop him from delivering life-saving goods like antifreeze to people in the high Arctic. The government tried to refuse Laserich a base of operations, but he got around that by carrying the bulk fuel. Willy was cited and fined a bunch of times before the government finally gave up and gave him the operating license. In the 1960s, he began transporting the sick and injured to hospitals sometimes more than 1,000 miles away, and by the early 1980s, the Laserich family started a medevac air ambulance company. One time, Laserich transported a woman with a large knife sticking straight out of her chest. The knife couldn't be removed for fear that she might bleed to death. The flight took place in a snowstorm where visibility was less than 45 feet, but they made it through.

I heard that story from Willy's teenage son Paul when I was growing up. Paul came to Alberta to get his pilot's license and became best friends with me and my sister Terry. Together we made one of our legendary road trips to Yellowknife. Paul was a great guy and he sure took after his old man. One day, my dad and I were working in the field when Paul appeared out of the sky and buzzed us low with his plane. He was so low that you could have just about jumped up and grabbed a wheel.

In the time before the ice roads, flying in the Arctic was dangerous and expensive. Even today, depending on the cargo, planes are three to eight times more expensive to operate than trucks. Engines iced up and shut down in midair, which forced pilots to control freefall plunges of thousands of feet. Emergency landings on frozen rivers were common, as were nights stranded on the tundra sometimes in axle-deep Muskeg swamp.

The planes had their limitations, and so did the Cat trains. They were cheaper to operate than the planes, but moved as slow as turtles. Each Cat weighed about 32,000 pounds and traveled at a top speed of 5 miles an hour, which earned them the nickname of "crawlers." Sometimes these trains would encounter pressure cracks on lakes, which, in turn, would form barriers up to 14 feet high that could stretch for miles in either direction. Equipment had to be carried to bridge such barriers. Crossing weak patches of virgin ice in these cumbersome behemoths was also a big risk. If the ice started to rupture, you couldn't drive yourself out of trouble. Meanwhile, once the ice broke, the Cat's massive weight was like a falling anvil. In fact, the trains frequently crashed through. And because there was often insufficient following distance between the Cats, sometimes more than one Cat would be lost in the same hole in the ice. In one instance, a lead Cat was pulling a cable 150 feet ahead of a bigger Cat, and behind that was a train of fifteen sleds. The lead Cat crossed a crack in the lake; however, the ice gave way under the heavier vehicle. The drivers couldn't cut the cable in time and the bigger Cat took the first down with it.

Statistics of the time are tough to come by; yet, of the four Cats embarking on a maiden trip to prove the viability of Cat trains, one cargo-laden vehicle sank to the bottom of the Athabaska River. The remaining three broke down repeatedly in the −40 temperatures. Eventually, three of the four Cats arrived in Yellowknife and the experiment was deemed a great success but a work in progress. That left only dog sleds, so by the late '50s and early '60s, you were still limited to hauling life essentials and maybe building materials like aluminum and lumber.

John Denison and his roads changed all that.

An ex-Mountie-turned-road-builder in Yellowknife, Big John, as he was known, stood six foot seven inches. Talk about long and lean. Denison is known as the father of the ice roads. Trained in mechanics, Denison joined the army during World War II. Following the war, he joined the Royal Canadian Mounted Police and was then attached to the RCMP in Yellowknife. A year later, in 1947, he suffered severe frostbite to his fingers, feet, and face during a massive search for a missing fur trapper on the Barren Lands. Denison soon resigned from the RCMP and left Yellowknife. Hunting for a new line of work, he arrived back in the Territories two years later. For a time, he worked on the Cat trains supplying mining camps with equipment. He eventually left to work with Byers Transport Limited, a hard-charging young trucking company that had recently begun daily service from Edmonton to Wainwright, Alberta.

Denison is often referred to as an engineer, but the truth is he didn't go to school to learn his profession. Completely self-taught through extensive trial and error, Denison had been stationed in Yellowknife and had seen firsthand the difficulties of moving goods. He was stubborn by nature and put little stock in conventional wisdom. He came to believe that trucks could do anything that a Cat train might, and so it was possible to make a winter road strong enough to support convoys of trucks hauling 40,000-pound loads over the ice. Of course, the good people of the Arctic thought he was crazy. It was one thing to drive a dogsled filled with diphtheria vaccine 50 miles in a whiteout; quite another to rely on a machine to do it.

Denison wasn't deterred. He had that hard-won skepticism that comes with living up North, but he also had a good dose of Northern ingenuity and he realized that the trick to making stronger and thicker ice was to expose it to air by removing the snow that acted as an insulator. Once the ice was open to the air, he reasoned, it would freeze from the bottom up and thicken. Driving over this ice would have the effect of pushing it down and then raising it up, which would expose it to even more air. But Arctic snow is too deep to just run a plow through, which is why Denison designed a way of dragging chains over the ice to take the air out of the snow.

Of course, this was back sixty years ago, when there were

few overland maps for Denison and his crew to go by. There was also nothing to tell him what was under the ice he was standing on. Everything was trial and error—hit or miss—and building his roads nearly finished Denison more than once.

Denison and his ice-road rangers went through real hardship in those early days. They were poorly equipped to face savage blizzards, whiteouts, and 60-below-zero temperatures. Steel axles snap like twigs in that kind of cold, and often the brakes and steering wheels will seize right up. The bare hands of the builders froze and fused as soon as they touched metal. The ice buckled and cracked and sometimes gave way. Because Denison's operation was self-funded and money was tight, most of the vehicles he used were castoffs. Some were more than twenty years old. This was at a time when the average life of a vehicle in the Arctic was two years. Worse, Denison only had one of each type of vehicle. He used a strange-looking amphibious vehicle with great big balloon tires, which he called "the beaver," for crew to sleep in as well as to transform rough terrain into portage roads between the over-water ice roads. He also had a Cat tractor that had to be towed from location to location by a truck; a camper truck with a trailer on the back for meals and sleeping; a massive truck called the *African Queen,* which had a lowboy trailer for hauling other vehicles, interchangeable caboose, and custom-designed snowplow in the front; a four-wheel-drive plow truck with a camper on it, called *Fud;* and a lightweight Bombardier "bug" with skis on the front so it could float.

When he built his road, Denison would lead the way with a plow attached to the front of his truck. He would bounce over stumps, rocks, and logs and every jag in the ice. If a vehicle broke down, his options were limited. If the problem was mechanical, either he would make a repair on site or send word back to a mechanic back in Yellowknife. Often, no replacement part existed, so the mechanic would have to fabricate a new one. This process could take several days, time that Denison didn't have. As his team made it farther and farther up the ice road, it grew exponentially more difficult to get help from Yellowknife. At a certain point, if something went wrong, there wasn't anyone to help for hundreds of miles. They had to rely on one another.

Every time a truck or machine crashed through the ice and went to the bottom, Denison had to find a way to haul it back up, dry it off, and get it going again. On Rae Lake, for example, three vehicles went through the ice. The lake featured islands that created narrow rocky shoals and blazing-fast currents. The resulting ice was notoriously unpredictable and full of potholes surrounded by weak ice. Denison had attempted to avoid Rae Lake entirely by taking an all-land portage route. However, the portage proved very rugged and difficult to navigate. Denison decided he had to risk cutting across the lake. The gamble didn't pay off. The team's Cat was the first to go in. It crashed through just 30 feet from shore. Luckily, the water was only 4 feet deep. Two trucks then broke the ice trying to retrieve the Cat. Luckily, they landed on shallow underwater rocks. None of the crew was killed, thank God, but no one would have blamed Denison if he abandoned the road and came home. People would have expected that. Instead, he brought in his cherry picker—a combination winch and hoist machine that looked like a giraffe and was capable of lifting heavy objects. It's hard to imagine the process of locating a submerged vehicle, locking onto it, and then pulling it back up even as the ice was reforming, but somehow Denison and his crew did it. Each operation took several hours. They recovered every one of the vehicles and continued on their way.

Denison and his team carved out more than 1,000 miles of ice roads in a single season. For doing all that he got the Order of Canada Medal, the nation's highest honor for outstanding merit or distinguished service. Ask anybody in those parts and they'll know that Denison was the guy who fought his way through blizzards and breakdowns to carve a 325-mile ice road from Yellowknife all the way to two destinations: Port Radium on the eastern shore of Great Bear Lake; and Coppermine on the Coronation Gulf, which sits above the Arctic Circle. It was those same ice roads that made way for the construction of oil field pipelines during the 1970s and 1980s—a huge step for the oil industry in the territory.

I knew Big John. Everybody in Yellowknife did. He was quite a character; in fact, he was a legend by the time I came along in the late '70s—old, but still hanging around. John was cantankerous as all get-out, but once you got to know him, you found that he had a hell of a sense of humor. And he could tell a story like nobody else. Of course, most of them were about getting stuck miles from help or falling through the ice in his truck. It was only after I started building and driving on the ice roads myself that I realized Denison was laughing about his own near-death experiences.

Sad to say, Denison is gone now, as are all the other pioneers. Some might look at us as his legacy, but those are mighty big shoes to fill. What we do is a walk in the park compared to what his kind endured. John wasn't philosophical about the ice roads. He'd tell you the way it was, but nothing about the lives he changed and the world he opened up. I don't know what he'd say if he saw the 11,000 loads we carry in a season. Anybody who whines about the roads now, well, they have no idea what they're even talking about. One ride on the Salmita road and they'd sing a different tune.

Some of the old Sno Cats and trucks from Denison's time are still being used. You still need them for accessing a big pile of gravel, rock, or sand that you can't reach until winter. So you build an ice road across a lake specifically for getting to the pile, and you take one of the old trucks with the plow on it and get her across. Once the ice has thickened, someone has to load the sand and haul it back for the summer supply. That's the kind of job I did when I first came to Yellowknife. After a day of hauling sand on the ice road, you'd go into a bar for a beer and there would be John Denison, sitting on a stool. He'd give a nod that meant it was fine to come over and tell him about the work you were doing on those old roads of his.

The roads that Denison built led to gold and silver mines

with names like Eldorado and Echo Bay, names that sounded as if they came out of adventure books. They offered adventure, that's for sure. There are dozens of abandoned gold mines around Yellowknife. Some are still capable of producing, but when the price of gold plummeted and they were no longer profitable to operate, the people who worked them just walked away, figuring that they'd come back when the prices went back up. Often the workers moved on and never came back. Even today you can see mines where the plates were left on dining-hall tables, and abandoned ambulance trucks sit waiting in garages. They've been forgotten by all except the old-timers.

In Denison's time, the roads were built with grit and spit. All you did was put a snowplow on the front of a loaded-down truck and away you went. By the time I started to drive, Denison's ice road route and even the mines he serviced were pretty much shuttered and gone. Discovery Mine was the last of them, and it closed in 2004. The ice roads they build now are farther east of Denison's and head up to Snap Lake and then on to Echo Bay and Tahera. I thought that my chance to drive a big rig on the actual Denison route had come and gone, but one night the opportunity came without warning.

It was storming worse than I had ever seen before, and a group of us barely limped into the camp at Lockhart, which is a main truck-stop located along the ice roads eight hours north of Yellowknife and midway to and from the most northern deliveries. Lockhart was a place to get a hot meal, take a load off, and park your truck for the night. Part of that group was my brother-in-law Paul, who was a newbie on the ice roads. He had just earned his Class 1 license and I had brought him up there to get his feet wet, so to speak. I was driving the Crow's Nest. Paul was driving my purple-and-white Freightliner.

Well, it was one in the morning and we had just spent several hours fighting our way through the storm. We felt fortunate to have made it to the camp. Having already delivered loads up north, we were all running empty, trying to make it back to the freight yards in Yellowknife to reload. The weather was not cooperating with that plan but might change in our favor. We figured we would eat and then decide what to do next. If it was humanly possible, I was going to head on back to Yellowknife. Paul figured he would sleep and head back when the roads were clear.

As hours passed, word began to trickle down that a team was being put together to take the old Denison road to Salmita gold mine. The Salmita had been closed for a long time; however, every time the price of gold went up, somebody would try to reopen it. Lots of times these were fly-by-night operations that would hastily construct the very crudest of ice roads using Sno Cats so that a single run of supplies could be sent to the mine. Typically, the deliveries are made, the Cats are retrieved, and then the road is closed, never to be opened again. Sometime in late spring or early summer, the would-be miners would arrive by barge or boat to open the mine. It costs the mine something like $30,000 to plow a road, which is why they only do it once. Usually, the company schedules a convoy of fourteen or fifteen trucks to go in at one time to make their haul.

The road construction crew had left two Sno Cats running and returned to town in a truck. Recovery of the Cats had been scheduled, but the bad weather had scrubbed that plan. At first, the company that owned the machines planned to wait out the snow, but the storm worsened by the hour. If the company waited much longer, the machines would quit or run out of fuel and then freeze solid. Restarting them would be very unlikely, which would make it impossible to load the 50,000-pound vehicles onto flatbeds for hauling out.

The proposed job sounded simple enough: Despite the storm, someone was needed to go to Salmita right away to grab the Cats and haul them out of there. So far, there were no takers. One look out the window at the storm and you could understand why.

Paul was on his way out the door to get some sleep, but I caught up with him.

"Do you want to come and make some more money?" I asked. He didn't. "Well, then, want to come with me on a ride you'll never forget?"

He was listening.

"The road has only been plowed for two days," I continued. "It's blowing and snowing like the end of the world. I don't know if I'll survive this one, but I know sure as hell that I'm going. This will be the ride of a lifetime."

Next thing you know, Paul was climbing back into his truck, but not to sleep.

Narrow, and rougher than a gravedigger's nut sack, Denison's roads were not easy even under the best of circumstances. This was not the best of circumstances. Before leaving, we topped off our fuel tanks, poured methyl hydrate into our brake and fuel lines, and stocked up on food and water just in case we got stuck. We did radio checks and made sure that dispatch knew where we were headed. We knew that if we got stopped by the storm, we would be stuck there for a couple of days.

The snowdrifts were as high as our trucks. We were boxed in on both sides. There was nothing but blackness beyond the small arc of our lights. The wind harassed us every foot of the way. I bludgeoned and knifed my way through snowdrifts piled high in front of my bumper. Sometimes I'd slam into a mound so hard that the snow would shoot high into the air. The road was deeply rutted and we swung hard back and forth with each jarring drop. The cab creaked and torqued even as the engine strained and roared. As we slowly rumbled and sledgehammered along, I told Paul, "Whatever you do, don't stop. Just keep coming no matter what. If you stop, you'll never get going again."

"Believe me, I'm gonna stick to you like white on rice," Paul said.

The roads had been made just two days earlier, which meant they hadn't been smoothed out with traffic. The snow was at least 2 feet deep (much deeper in some places), and the road was only as wide as a Cat. The Cat had plowed through once, so we had the tracks to follow, but they were already full of drifts, which meant that we could drive at about 15 and no faster than 20 miles an hour. I expected real trouble handling corners, so all our lockers were on to give us some control over how fast our tires would rotate. Without our lockers on, we would literally be spinning our wheels. With the lockers, if a tire hits an icy spot and needs to work harder than an adjacent wheel that may not be under the same degree of stress, that tire can spin faster to essentially keep pace. Locked and loaded, we hoped it was just a matter of going head-down and ass-up, driving as fast and carefully as we could.

We soon saw that the road was rougher and more un-even than we had imagined. You'd bang and bounce hard to the left and then ride at an angle on the right with one side of the truck up on a 15-degree angle. We were going over ice, but also over portages and tundra that were roads in name only.

When you plow through a snowdrift first, and then it drifts in again, it's like hitting cement. If I'm the first one through a snowdrift, then it's still soft. I knew that as long as I hammered down, I could make it through. Our heads were banging the roofs of the trucks all the way. Sometimes the front of the truck would go airborne and crash down hard. Luckily, we never broke anything. There was so much snow, you wouldn't see a boulder or fallen tree until it was too late.

I called Paul on the radio. "There are some big drifts up here that are higher than the hood," I told him. I'd accelerate to plow through them Denison-style. Afterward, I'd say into the radio, "I made it, so just put your foot into it." Paul did as I told him, but he kept shouting, "Holy fuck! We're not going to get out of here! Holy fuck!!!" I must have heard that phrase coming out of his mouth two hundred times. He was hollering at me on the radio the whole way. As for me, I was shouting at the storm and the drifts: "Oh, yeah? Is that your best, you son of a bitch? What else have you got???"

Paul thought we were out of our minds. He may have been right. There wasn't another soul on the road. I wasn't sure exactly where we were going, but we kept moving. I wasn't going to stop until we found the mine or ran out of road.

Out of the darkness, the mine's head shaft rose up about five stories against the dark sky. Somehow we had made it, but with snow swirling in the wind and no signs of life, the Salmita Mine was as eerie as a ghost town. We quickly realized that there was no one there. The snow kept falling, which gave the place a look like something out of *The Shining*.

The snowdrifts were up past our windows. The wind was ferocious. I grabbed my gloves and kicked the door open with all of my might. The snow was mountainous and you had to catch your breath just moving through it. The scar tissue in my lungs wouldn't let me get enough air. I could barely breathe. I didn't say a word to Paul, but he looked worried.

The convoy had come and gone before the storm hit, but there were the two Sno Cats left behind, and we had to figure out how to get them out of there. We were there another two hours building ramps so we could get the Sno Cats onto the truck flatbeds. Paul was terrified that we would never get out.

"Listen," I told him. "I got us in and I'll get us out of here."

We finally got both Sno Cats loaded, and I said, "Now comes the fun part. These Cats have fourteen-and-a-half-foot-wide blades. We'll be lucky to have about twelve feet of clearance so we're sure to hit snowbanks on both sides. It will be like that the whole way back." Paul's face just dropped. I said, "It's the same thing coming back: hammer down and don't stop no matter what." We strapped the Cats down with chains, knowing the plows would be hitting and plowing the snowbanks on the way out.

Going back, we rammed and slammed even harder than before. A few times, it looked like we were going to be stuck. We would have been stranded for days. Who would come for us in this weather? We just pushed away the snow with the big rigs and plowed the road wider with the Cats. Eight hours after we started, at nine o'clock in the morning, we made it all the way back to Lockhart in time for breakfast. It was surreal. Nobody was in the camp. The storm had passed and work had begun. Paul and I toasted with coffee cups. Soon we would be on the road again. It was just another day.

5

A MILE A DAY

 drove on the ice for the first time in 1981. I was nineteen. My employer was RTL, owned by Dick Robinson, and the trip was to the Discovery Mine, 50 miles east of Yellowknife. What I remember most about that drive was the thinness of the fresh ice and the noise it made under my bumper. I was certain that the ice was about to break and this trip would be my first and last.

RTL gave me a 1973 White Western Star to drive, a plain Jane that had seen better days. The weather-beaten cover of the manual had a little caption that read "We build your White Western Star like it's the only one you own." That's true, because once you drove one of those rickety old trucks, you never wanted to own another. There was no heat, no sleeping compartment, and no radio except a CB with a signal range of about 5 miles. The truck had wipers, but I generally used an ice scraper to see out of the little portholes

I struggled to keep clear. Bundled up in my rabbit-fur hat, heavy gloves, and insulated snowmobile suit, I would drive with one hand and scrape with the other. The trip was a short haul—two and a half hours each way.

Back then, the science of building ice roads and monitoring their safety was primitive. To test the ice, someone would head out onto a lake, drill a few holes with an auger, and declare, "This road is fine." That was it. Of course, it might be fine in that particular spot, but not thick enough thirty feet away. The road would be opened, and a little while later somebody would go through. Part of the problem was that loads weren't weighed in relation to the time of the season or the capacity of the ice. We were flying blind without parachutes.

Things have changed since then. Now the entire ice road system costs $35 million to build every season. That works out to be more than $100,000 per mile. It's a lot of money, that's for sure, but the roads must be strong and suitable for all kinds of vehicles and all kinds of loads, from pickups to double eighteen-wheelers—what we call B-trains or super-Bs. These super-B monsters have load capacities of more than 180,000 pounds, the maximum weight allowed on the roads.

From year to year no two ice roads are exactly the same. For starters, the quality of the roads are fine-tuned each year, which involves straightening, smoothing rough patches, and widening—especially on the portages. Meanwhile, the routes themselves change according to the base ice provided by Mother Nature. The sometimes vast bodies of water on which the ice sits are flowing, shifting, and moving with the currents, so a route that was ideal last year now may be unsafe. That lack of consistency is what makes building on the ice even more dangerous than driving on the ice. Some of the lakes are so big that when you're on them you can't see the beginning, sides, or end. There are no land markers, just an ocean of white in every direction. Somehow you have to plow a road across snow-buried ice that you can't even see.

How do you know where to go?

The only thing to guide you are the sometimes half-buried Hägglunds or Bombardier tracks made the day before in front of you. You're sitting on a Cat that weighs 45,000 pounds and you better hope that the radar guiding those tracks is nothing less than 100 percent accurate. You're out there in the middle of nowhere, and if you suddenly break through no one will come to your aid for hours. Virgin ice can shatter like crystal and take you down like an anchor before you have a chance to stand up in your seat. That's a scary-ass concept to wrap your head around. Talk about guts.

At least if my truck goes down, length and weight displacement of the vehicle will slow down the descent enough to give me a chance to react. Plus, there's a good chance that another truck will happen along within a couple of minutes.

Of course, there's one and only one reason why the ice roads get built: money. Huge multinationals are hunting gold, diamonds, and oil, and they need the roads to service the hunt. If you can stand temperatures that can be 70 below zero, and cold that snaps metal like twigs, then you have a chance of striking your own bonanza or making your own fortune. Road-building companies like Nuna Logistics and

RTL start mapping out the ice roads as early as July, when the ice has melted and the bodies of water are fully revealed. Float planes and helicopters are brought in to study the terrain and locate underwater reefs, shoals, and currents. An incredible amount of data is collected, with changes from the previous year particularly noted. Only then are the potential winter road routes mapped out and construction methods specific to each section chosen.

Beginning in late October and early November, when the mercury plunges and Old Man Winter kicks it into high gear on the tundra, crews from Nuna Logistics and RTL will fan out from Tibbitt Lake up to Contwoyto more than 350 miles away. They'll work around the clock to construct a mile of road each day.

The roads are a feat of modern engineering and Old World guts. First, helicopters equipped with ground-penetrating radar measure ice thickness over an entire body of water. If the ice is determined to be safe, a light track-vehicle like a Hägglunds, an amphibious track machine made in Sweden for military use, is brought in to scout the area with GPS to revalidate ice thickness. The Hägglunds are basically ATV work horses that go anywhere. No special license, certification, or training is required; however, anyone who lives in the North is very familiar with ATVs. They can easily operate in temps as cold as 40 below and zip and bound across the tundra at 40 miles an hour. The Hägglunds are light and quick and able to go just about anywhere. They're one of the most versatile vehicles on the planet. If the ice breaks under them, they're able to float. They even come equipped with escape hatches.

Track machines like the Bombardier, with balloon tires 34 to 72 inches wide, are part of the advance team. They're used for transportation, plowing, and grading. (When it comes to vehicles and equipment, the more displaced the weight, the better.) In addition to having giant tires, these vehicles are also relatively light. They can work on undeveloped ice in the early stages of road-building with less chance of breaking through. Because of their weight and wide tracks, the Bombardiers are also easier on freezing muskeg in the small portions of road that are over land. Come springtime, when the roads will melt to nothing, they won't damage the tundra.

When the ice thickens, heavier machines like trucks and snowplows are brought in to re-plow and widen the roads or build up the snowbanks that will prevent drivers from veering onto the surrounding lake or river ice that may be unsafe. The construction teams compact the snow already on the ice. Next, tanker trucks drop either seawater from the ocean, if they're up in Inuvik (which is on the East Channel of the Arctic Ocean's Mackenzie Delta), or freshwater from nearby lakes if they're out of Yellowknife. They simply drill holes into the ice with augers and pump water to the surface. One mile of ice road requires 1 to 1.5 million gallons of water to create 6 inches of ice with a width of 40 feet. A water truck holding 3,000 to 4,000 gallons sprays water evenly over a section to form a firm crust. (This isn't the environmental nightmare that it appears to be. The water used to make ice is pumped up from the lake or river on which you're building the road. Come springtime, it will melt and return to its previous state. Extensive analysis is conducted in the summer to ensure that the water has returned to its pristine condition with no lasting residue.)

After the water is sprayed and the crust is formed, chipped or crushed ice is then laid down to build up the thickness of the ice and create a smooth surface. The crushed ice is watered down so that it freezes. This process is repeated until the ice road reaches a certain thickness—at least 16 inches. Next, a road grader is brought in. These engineering machines are equipped with long blades used to scar the surface of the ice. The scarring creates traction, an essential feature for the trucks. The colder it gets, the better the traction. That's because colder temperatures create more brittle ice on the surface.

The vast majority of ice roads are built over water and the remaining are over land. Between two bodies of water, you'll have the little islands of land, the portages. The terrain is usually very rugged, so temporary roads must be constructed here, too. Here, you'll see Cats plowing, felling trees, skidding, and digging. Road builders will bulldoze a trail that will be as narrow as 20 feet across, then they'll flood the space. Sand is added before the water can freeze, to create a slurry of mudlike sand and water that will harden into a sort of Arctic concrete. Many of the portages are steep and uneven. You'll bruise the crown of your head and rattle the fillings out of your teeth driving over them if you're not careful.

To speed up the construction process, the road builders use two ice-profiling teams to measure the thickness and variation of the ice: one team on the north end and another team working from the south. The teams work nonstop and meet mid-route to finish off the roads. It's a lot like the way they built railroads in the American Old West.

Profiling and measuring the ice has become a closely guarded science unto itself. Thickness of ice, proximity to reefs and shorelines, the weight of individual loads, speeds of the trucks, and the following distance between vehicles are all subject to precise mathematical calculations. Any errors in the formula can result in underwater tidal waves strong enough to cause pressure blowouts that rupture the ice and send drivers to their deaths. The ice road builders must determine not only ice thickness and temperature, which can change over time, but also how a specific section of ice may react to various conditions. For example, a patch of ice built up near irregular underwater terrain like a shoal with a strong cross-current may not deflect under the weight of a truck load in the same way as another patch located nearby. Companies like RTL have developed computer programs that can test the ice, incorporating variables such as speed, weight, following distance, water movement, and temperature.

Nuna Logistics and RTL are constantly maintaining the roads with their special trucks equipped with ground-penetrating radar. Even in the worst weather, you'll see the crews out there, filling in the cracks, plowing the snow drifts, checking to make sure everything is okay. Safety is a major concern for everyone involved with the ice roads. 2007 was a record year with nearly eleven thousand hauls made by more than six hundred trucks, yet there were only nine accidents and only one minor injury.

Safety enforcement plays a big part in that success. That's where SecureCheck comes in. SecureCheck security staff are on the road twenty-four hours a day, seven days a week. Their little white pickup trucks are a common sight on the ice. In 2007, the seventeen-member security staff logged 168,000 miles patrolling the roads, using radar to clock speeds and set up speed traps. Unsafe practices by truckers can result in verbal and written warnings, and eventually five- and seven-day suspensions. In extreme situations, a driver might even get banned from the ice roads. In 2007, there were 120 infractions.

When the roads are operational, dispatchers from Yellowknife will control truck traffic to regulate the number of vehicles on the ice at any given time. Rigs are prohibited from traveling on the ice alone and must maintain half a mile of spacing in between them. Generally, three trucks are dispatched from the yard every twenty minutes. Weights are monitored. Heavy and wide loads are dispatched between midnight and 6:00 a.m. to avoid daily commuter traffic, which is anyone leaving their home and driving on the Ingraham to get to work. The Ingraham is a regular asphalt road that leads to the ice roads. Anyone who lives in and around Yellowknife can drive on it, which makes for a dicey situation, especially in bad weather when small personal vehicles mix it up with our heavily laden big rigs. Big rigs and double-sized super-Bs with 60-ton loads don't mix well with the distracted drivers of little SUVs. Nowhere is that more apparent than in the Arctic.

Speed kills on the ice roads, so drivers with loads are

restricted to speeds no greater than about 20 miles per hour. Trucks running empty or without loads can travel faster, about 30 miles per hour, depending on the road and conditions. Holes are drilled to check the thickness of the ice. If some extra "paving" is required, the water trucks come out. For unknown reasons, sometimes ice doesn't set properly in a particular spot. There may be a rogue underwater current or a sandbar, it's hard to say. If the road can't be rerouted, the engineers will scratch their heads for a bit before bringing in a rig mat. These lattices of steel and wooden beams are frozen into the ice to bridge a weak spot. The fix is temporary and the crews will keep an eye on it.

Nuna Logistics and RTL check the ice every day with profilograph systems that use ground-penetrating radar to measure the thickness of the ice. It's a real science, so if they say the road is safe, you trust them and you drive. We sure have come a long way from the early days of traveling over these roads.

6

EVERY MAN FOR HIMSELF

verybody has a story about their worst storm. Mine took place in 1991. It was 4:00 in the morning when I left Yellowknife. I was loaded down, hauling shockrete, a type of cement that you spray on mine walls to toughen them up and make the shaft more stable. I was headed about 350 miles north to the Jericho Mines when I heard the broadcast that a storm was coming. The weather service is pretty good with their predictions. They said this was going be a bad one—a real doozy—and usually they're right on the money. I figured I had forty-eight hours before the storm hit, that I could be up there and back safe in about forty-two to forty-four hours. At least that's what I figured.

Six or seven hours into the trip, I came to where some rookie had spun out on Portage 25, what we call Charlie Hill.

Portages can be rough and the grade uneven. Lots of times, one shoulder is high and you're in a gully on the other, so you're basically clawing your way through. If you don't know how to drive—if you don't know how to pull a load up there—you'll spin out every time, guaranteed. You're beat, then, because you can't go anywhere. Without the benefit of your trailer to push you through, you and your load are dead weight, and you'll need a towline to pull you out. That can take hours. Pretty soon, you'll have a shitload of trucks backed up at the bottom. The trucks aren't moving, so the truckers aren't making money and they're all screwed. The drivers get pretty irritated, especially when they're under the gun and a little tired. To make matters worse, trucks should never stop out on the ice because the road isn't meant to hold a static load. Trucks that are sitting are pushing out hot exhaust and maybe leaking fluids, like oil, all of which can get at the ice. The trick is not to grab a gear where you've got lots of power. Instead, you grab a gear where you've got momentum. That way, you don't have enough power to spin, but you have enough power to pull a load over the hill.

Because Charlie Hill is really just a goat trail wide enough for one truck, you've got to hit her hard at the bottom of the hill and hope like hell you make her to the top. But let's say you're going in, and there's another guy running empty on the other side. He's supposed to stop. But let's say he doesn't hear you—well, then you bust mirrors and scrape trucks all the way through the portage. Only you might be loaded with 60 tons that has to stay balanced at all times. You'd come out the other side and be glad you were still alive.

This rookie was pulling a B-train full of fuel and he'd spun out—jackknifed across the hill. So there we sat for more than four hours while this damn newbie kept trying to straighten out his rig. He had the road all chewed up. It was a hell of a mess. Finally, a cab came and pulled him out of the way. Then they had to fix the holes in the road. That was about four hours. By now, one hundred trucks were backed up, waiting to get going. And the storm was coming.

I missed the rest stop. I figured I better just carry on. Stopping for a meal or rest would have just put me back another hour, so I kept on going. I made it up there to the Jericho Mines and got unloaded. Next, I filled up with fuel in case I got stranded heading back. And I got a few sandwiches. By now, time was against me, but I hit the road anyway. If I holed up every time a storm came through, I'd be out of business for sure. When you're running hard, it's easy to forget to eat and drink. But if you do, the cold will catch up with you real quick and leave you dehydrated and tired just when you need to be sharp. Dehydration is a real problem the colder it gets. I carry gallons of water in my truck at all times. I'll drink a gallon of water every run. That's in twenty-four hours. Of course, then you'll be peeing off the patio—stepping out onto the running board of the moving truck and with one hand still on the wheel. You take care of any other personal business like bowel movements at the camps so you time it for eight-hour intervals. If you eat something that doesn't sit right and you get diarrhea, that's your baby and you have to deal with it. Some will have a port-a potty just for emergencies. I've also seen truckers driving along, bare-assed and relieving themselves on the ice while holding onto the door handle. That calls for the air horn.

I had only made it about 50 kilometers out of the mine—about 30 miles—when the storm hit. It was blowing and snowing real bad, but I just kept on going as hard as I could. The snow was getting deeper and deeper. I gripped the steering wheel as hard as I could and barreled through. The engine roared, but pretty soon my truck wouldn't move forward. Not an inch. I was stuck, all right. I just sat there with nothing but the wind howling away. It blew and rocked that truck back and forth.

Most of the time, we go in packs or convoys, so maybe fifteen or sixteen trucks get stopped in one spot. But I was hauling a single load alone, and that was a bad thing. And that would be the last road to get plowed—they have to get everybody so they can get mobile farther down south, from mine to mine, from camp to camp. So that was the last road to get plowed out—the road where I was stranded. Sure as shit, I was on my own. But they knew I was up there, and that was the main thing. They come and get you sooner or later.

Back then, all we had were CBs. The radios only go so far, and they didn't even go over hills. I was out of range of any other human being, for sure. Outside, it was pushing 60 below and the wind was maybe 50 to 60 miles an hour. I've been out in the bush lots of times where I had to stay there and build a fire, and figure out where I was in the morning. My sense of direction is pretty good no matter where I am. I figure that if I pay attention to where I'm going, I'll always find a way back.

But this was a whiteout, and if you get out of the truck, it's easy to get disoriented. You'd freeze to death in minutes. The cold would freeze the blood right out of your face, arms, and legs. Your skin would turn white like the snow. I lost the tip of a finger this way. Another driver lost his toes and had to learn how to walk again. Frostbite happens before you even know it. You don't even get a pain warning. That's why they like anyone who has a job outside to work in pairs. That way, you can keep an eye on each other. I figured they knew that I was somewhere between two places—they knew that because I hadn't checked in anywhere else. And they knew I was on my way back, so they would send guys out on track machines—Sno Cats. They come out and check on you to make sure you're all right, and so that they know that some-body's there. So you stay in the truck, unless you jump out to piss.

People always think there's something special about the trucks we drive, but there isn't. You put whatever you want on them—the tires, the weather lines, all that kind of stuff. This truck was an '84 International, which was nothing like the trucks we have nowadays.

I kept the truck running at 1,200 rpm's, not only to keep warm, but because the engine would freeze solid pretty quick otherwise. If the engine freezes up, you're pretty much done. You've got about fifteen minutes to get that truck running if it's stopped. Once the block freezes, there's nothing you can do about it. You better get it started again in fifteen minutes or that's it. Besides the truck's heater, I had a sleeping bag rated for 60 below. While the storm kept at it, I just sat there and ate and drank what I had. Pretty soon, my truck and trailer were completely entombed in snow. The wind, and the truck creaking and groaning, were the only sounds I could hear. They never let up.

I'd been doing this my whole life. I've been in snowstorms where I've been stranded for days on end, and whiteouts, too. So it wasn't a question of being scared or anything. Out here, if you worry about dying, that's the best way to end up dead. The only one you can count on to save your ass is yourself, so you better keep your head on straight.

The only thing that I really thought about was what the worst thing that could happen was. Maybe I'm going to run out of fuel, my truck will quit, and it'll freeze up. I wouldn't have much of a chance if it did. But I know they're coming sooner or later. They're coming because they've got a truck missing. Everybody has a truck number and that number didn't show up somewhere. So a truck—my truck—is missing.

Again, the most important thing to remember is keep your truck running and don't get out. Never *ever* leave your equipment, because that is your lifeline—your only lifeline. Even if you figure help is just down the road, you can't get out and walk. You have to stay in your truck. Guys have become disoriented from the lack of visibility and the cold, and have frozen to death only 150 feet from safety. Besides, there are animals up there. Wolverines, polar bears, and packs of wolves roam about. Polar bears and wolves will kill and eat you without thinking twice. You're easy to catch and nice and crunchy as far as they're concerned. A male polar bear can stand up to 12 feet high and easily weigh more than 1,000 pounds. There have been some that weighed as much as 2,000 pounds. You don't stand a chance. Same goes for a pack of wolves or a lone wolverine. In fact, if the truck has sat for a while, you never know if some wolverine has made a camp under your truck. It happened to me once during another whiteout.

I was in mid-piss off the second step of my truck when I heard this awful hiss come from underneath the cab. Wolverines are the nastiest, most aggressive animals on earth. They're capable of taking a kill away from wolves. Even grizzly bears won't mess with them. They'll attack you just to attack you, and there I was, face-to-face with one. Turns out it had made a den under the truck and had no idea that I was there. I must have scared it just enough for me to jump back in the cab quick and phone the game officer. Luckily, they were able to trap it and release it back into the tundra. No one got hurt. Not me. Not the wolverine. I've had times where wolverines were trapped by a high snowbank. Once a wolverine turned around and stood up, baring its teeth and claws. It wanted to fight with my truck. It actually attacked it.

In a whiteout, your best bet is to just sit inside, bide your time, and hope to hell somebody comes, the sooner the better. There was a little box that I had in that International. It was just one little cubbyhole that you would flop yourself through and have a little nap. That's about all I could do. With the storm banging away, mostly I conserved energy and slept, so that I could go hard again. You get about three blizzards a month up there in the winter. During the season, you could expect to lose a couple days of work. So if I'm not broke down, I catch up on my sleep. Then I'm fresh. I'm ready to go kick some ass again.

I don't need a lot of sleep. Even as a kid, I never needed more than five or six hours of sleep. On the road, lots of times I've had to stay up for well over thirty hours at a crack. You just persevere. You make yourself stay awake. Open your windows or do whatever you gotta do to stay awake. You jump out on the running board when you're driving and freeze your ass off for a minute and get back in and warm up. All kinds of stuff. I've gone thirty-five hours straight, running until I couldn't stay awake anymore. Even after thirty-five hours, I still only needed five or six hours before I was ready to go again.

The whole time, the cab of my truck was whipsawed by the wind. It was at least thirty-six hours before anybody got a hold of me. By then, you couldn't even see me, but I sure as hell was in the truck. They came, plowed, and pulled me out. From all the rocking back and forth by the wind, my wheels now sat on wedges of snow 18 inches off the ground. But the situation was over. Down I went to the next base, filled up with fuel, and was back on the haul. Just like that, it was another day at work. On the ice road, there's a thin line between what happened, what didn't happen, and what could have happened. That difference can determine whether or not you make it.

Every Man for Himself

Everything in the North is a race against the clock—a race to beat a storm, a race to beat the change of seasons, a race to hunker down before the roads go out. You've only got three months of summer, so you've got to plan ahead and do as much as you can ahead of time. You can't expect to come up here in January and just make a deal for the season. If you want a job, you need to apply early—that means approaching the truck company the summer before. And you can't just show up with your rig and head out onto the ice roads, either. You've got to have an assignment from a company that does winter road runs, or you've got to be an owner-operator with your own contracts to deliver to remote communities. I fall into that second category. Me and my four rigs.

But I'm only one driver, and more than six hundred will be hired for the upcoming season. Canadian citizenship is a major priority since work visas must be obtained for foreign workers, which can be a long and painstaking process. Next comes a clean driving and criminal record, as well as a track record of experience, especially on roads that see a lot of snow and ice.

Experienced ice road truckers share a "Get 'er done" attitude that a driver who has moved from company to company will lack. That attitude is crucial to success on the winter road, where a driver may be unmonitored and on his own for days at a time. The freight companies will look for that attitude in prospective drivers. Finally, although you need not be a mechanic, it's important to be able to troubleshoot and have contingencies for all the mechanical breakdowns an ice road driver can expect to face. Given the conditions we work in, it's amazing that any machine we operate works, so you can't expect them to function perfectly or at all 100 percent of the time. A good driver will thoroughly check and recheck his equipment before and after every delivery. He learns to anticipate problems. A driver who cuts corners or doesn't have the right know-how regarding his engine will very quickly be sidelined. Even a breakdown of a day or two can cost the company thousands of dollars, so basic mechanical competency is something employers require.

Successful ice road drivers are observant and detail-oriented, and have a workmanlike attitude. You'll notice that I never mentioned "daredevil." Drivers whose primary qualification is "I live for danger!" can risk their necks someplace else, because no Arctic freight company will hire them.

Every January, I get a cartage contract from the freight-hauling company, which spells out the process, terms, payment rates, cost, and reimbursements of delivering—literally "carting"—cargo. The contract runs eight or ten pages and is filled with legalese that defines their liability (zero), various rules and regs, and grounds for breach and termination. Particularly worth mentioning, a driver can be responsible for damage or loss of goods, which can be a sobering thought when you realize that some of our freight would cost millions of dollars to replace. Of course, I have insurance for that; however, such insurance does not cover incidents of gross negligence.

I sign the contract; then I can hire drivers for my other three trucks. I get paid by the freight company a rate per delivery. Anybody who drives one of my trucks gets a percentage of that rate, paid out by me at the end of the season. I give an advance to each driver as a show of good faith, so I'm always starting my season in a hole, running a deficit until I start making money on the road. The freight companies have no liability for me or my drivers, so it's on me to cover everybody. It's my skin that's on the hook if anybody, including me, gets hurt, so I make sure I have the best insurance possible. I literally have to cover each trip on the ice, which is how cost is calculated. I don't mind hiring newbies, because you can build them up from scratch and teach them good habits. Often they want to prove they can make it, so they don't whine. Pull your weight. That's my only rule.

I've always found that it's best to drive the 1,900 miles to Yellowknife in a pack, so my drivers and I will head out from Kelowna together. My shop is right across the way from my house. I can walk out my door and be at work on my trucks in thirty seconds. My drivers will meet me at the shop just before sunrise on the big day. Usually, they're pretty excited, nervous and chatty as kids in a schoolyard. This is my last chance to look them in the eye and say, "Listen, if you have any personal problems or any other reason you can't focus on what we're about to do, don't you dare leave this yard in my truck." None have stepped out of the lineup, but you can see them sober up quick.

Mornings can be cold and clear, heavy with fog, or snowing. If we're really lucky, the sun will be splashing its first light across the mountain. I've done everything there is to do to set up the trucks, so all the drivers have left is to stow their gear. My rig, the Crow's Nest, was packed the day before, so I go to my big freezer in the shop, which is where I keep all the meat from animals I've shot during hunting season. There might be deer, elk, or bear in there. I'll pull out a hind section of, say, wild boar, and saw off a big hunk to give to my dog, Scrappy. "That should hold you till I get back," I'll tell him. After that, my wife and I will say our good-byes. She hates for me to leave and always worries, but after so many years, she knows the drill.

I give her my best polar-bear hug, and around that time you can bet that at least one of the drivers will blow his horn and shout, "Why don't you two go get a room?" I climb into my rig and, with the other three trucks following, away we go. If I check my side mirror fast enough, I can see Dianne crossing the driveway and going back into the house. Sometimes I'll catch a glimpse of Scrappy burying his boar meat in the snow. The piece will be twice the size of his head and he'll have his work cut out for him.

It feels like a million bucks to get under way. All the anticipation and excitement has been building like a volcano inside me for the last couple of months and now we're actually doing it. I can feel the rumble of the road coursing through my hand on the shifter and in my foot on the accelerator. There's no place I'd rather be, because the ice road has been built for me and I am built for this road. Every bad patch of ice, every bump, twist, and turn will be like a reunion with an old friend.

"Goddamn, I can't wait to get at her, boys!" I say over the radio. "Soon we'll be making *money!*"

It doesn't all run smoothly, though. Once, I had a driver go off the road just minutes after leaving Kelowna, which has some mountain driving. That's no way to start a season. The road was glazed in places with ice, and some of the turns were shrouded in mountain fog. Such conditions can pose a challenge to most drivers, but compared to what you see out on the ice, they're child's play. Still, winter road driving doesn't mean you can be cavalier; it means knowing when to be cautious and pay attention. In this particular instance, the driver was unfamiliar with the section of road and took his eye off the ball. Down into the ditch he went. If a driver talks the talk and claims to have a certain level of experience, and his references check out, unfortunately, there's no way to see what he's really made of until he's actually out there and driving. I had to pull this particular driver out myself. I remember that he muttered some excuses about the fog, the ice, and the grade while looking down at his boots. I just cut him off. I said, "You're supposed to be able to handle this stuff. What the hell are you going to do when you're driving on the real deal?" Some drivers need a good scare to get with the program and up to speed, and that's what I hoped in this case.

But usually, the start isn't nearly so eventful. Kelowna to Edmonton by way of Jasper is just highway driving, and there's nothing complicated about it except for keeping an eye out for cops. "Watch your speed, boys," I'll say. We'll make the 560 miles in about ten hours.

In Edmonton, I give my drivers what I call "the last hurrah dinner." I treat everybody to a big, juicy steak and lots of beer. This is the chance for everybody to get to know one another. There will be plenty of time to discuss the ice roads, so I try to keep the guys' minds off of that. Mostly, we just have a good time and don't discuss the ice roads. A hockey game will be on at the bar and we might watch and relax. It's funny. Hockey may be Canada's national pastime, but it's the one sport I never played. Many tykes start as soon as they can stand up, but we were too poor to buy skates. By the time I had my own money, the chance to learn had pretty much passed me by. These days, my schedule on the ice roads conflicts with the hockey season, so I miss most games unless my teams, Edmonton or Calgary, make it to the playoffs. I love NASCAR, and that's a sport I stay on top of every week. I guess driving is just in my blood. To each his own, eh?

When you get north of Edmonton, you'll see fewer and fewer people. It fact, it's downright desolate. At one time, you could drive for an hour without seeing another vehicle in either direction. Nowadays, that happens less and less, but the road still seems desolate and forbidding to anyone who doesn't have a memory of the old days. Cell-phone coverage is still nearly nonexistent though, so frequent travelers to this area carry satellite phones in case of emergency.

The 970-mile stretch of the Mackenzie Highway didn't even exist until the late 1940s and even then, about two-thirds of it was gravel. The road was a mine field of potholes and ruts sometimes 2 and 3 feet deep. Cats were used to tow vehicles through the worst sections. The trip was so daunting that travelers took to calling their destination in Yellowknife "The Promised Land." As recently as two years ago, large sections were still gravel and you were guaranteed to lose a windshield and wear out your mud flaps on every trip. Even today part of the road is a roller-coaster ride made even more challenging by the bison herds that wander across and are especially hard to see at night.

In the early nineteenth century, upward of 80 million bison, or American buffalo, roamed the Americas from Alaska to Northern Mexico. By the end of the 1800s, fewer than 300 remained. Seen as a nuisance to railroads, ranchers, and homesteaders in the United States, buffalo were all but eradicated both in the United States and Canada. It's a story known to every schoolkid. Luckily, in the early 1900s, the Canadian government had the foresight to buy some of the last American herds in Montana before it was too late. Today, there are more than 225,000 bison in Canada. Most are privately owned. Of those, half are located in Alberta, where they roam over giant tracts of open land in herds numbering in the hundreds and sometimes thousands. Buffalo meat is extremely nutritious and low in calories. It's one of the most tasty red meats, too. I'd eat it every day if I had to. Besides its domestic consumption, bison meat is exported around the world, especially to France and the United States.

For the final nearly 200 miles from Fort Providence to Yellowknife, there are no gas stations. If you don't gas up in Fort Providence, you can find yourself in a lot of trouble, especially in winter. In the old days, small-vehicle drivers carried several 5-gallon containers of gas to make it through. You were guaranteed to use them. That's what my sister and I did as teenagers when we made the trek in her little Vega station wagon back in the late '70s. Nowadays, many travelers still carry extra fuel in case of emergency. Of course, no self-respecting truck driver would ever be caught dead running out of fuel. I fill up before every trip no matter how short. My trucks all have twin 150- or 175-gallon tanks. I can sit out a storm idling for four days. Running empty, I can go a max of 3,000 miles on those two tanks. Road grades and conditions, and whether you're hauling freight, all factor in to how far you can go.

Next to gas, insect repellent is a must. There are many spectacular waterfalls all along the way, but the bugs are ferocious except in late autumn and winter. Woe to any traveler who gets out of a vehicle without repellent. Clouds of biting insects will swarm and pursue you. I've seen people get bitten dozens of times in a minute.

I usually have to make one or two solo drives a year—once in the summer, or, if I don't do it then, in December, just before the season starts and I have to take the trucks up in January. I'll drive up in my pickup to get everything organized. I have a storage unit with extra chains, boomers, tow lines, tires, brake pads, belly pads, heater switches, belts, and hoses. Basically, if the weather can get at it, I have a replacement. I check the condition of everything and make sure it's in good working order and ready for the winter roads. Some seasons have ended with me delivering a load and then heading straight home to beat a storm. If something needs replacing, it's easier and cheaper to find parts down south now than to wait for a breakdown during the season. I like to show my face and renew friendships, but I'm really there for my equipment. It's also good to spend time with my sister Terry. We'll have dinner and maybe go hunting or fishing together.

On my solo drives, I usually drive straight through. I'll make that 1,900 miles in twenty-four hours in my pickup truck and in thirty hours in a big rig, 63 and 50 miles per hour, respectively. That may sound like a lot of miles in a short amount of time but it isn't anything special for a trucker. When I'm driving up with the guys, it will take us about thirty-eight hours, because of the dinner, sleep, and stopping for breakfast. We'll yak on the radio quite a bit and it will be an easy, relaxing drive.

When we get to Yellowknife, I take the guys out for supper and I show them around. Both the meal and tour are all business. "This is the time for questions," I'll say. The guys will have a free afternoon or even a whole day now and again to figure out where to do their laundry, send mail, buy groceries and cigarettes, and do their banking. A few guys might even want a night in a real bed, so I show them a hotel or two, just in case. Most of the guys have big plans at the start of the season, such as going hunting or ice fishing, seeing the local sights, or learning a thing or two about local life. But they rarely get past the bars.

Many of the local residents are oblivious to what goes on out on the ice just outside of town, and most drivers quickly become unaware of anything beyond life on the road and storm alerts. Sometimes you'll hear about something that happened in Yellowknife, like a fire, which is a common occurrence even in winter because of the huge propane- and oil-storage tanks each building must have to heat and run everything. But it might as well be something that happened a thousand miles away. A crash or a man going down on the ice feels similarly remote to residents not involved in the day-to-day operation of the roads, or whose livelihoods aren't dependent on what we do.

The bars of Yellowknife are the stuff of legend. Some have even had songs written about them. Places like the West Spot (which burned down), the Monkey Tree, the Gallery, the Discover Inn, Harley's, and the infamous Gold Range. Even back in the '70s, there were lots of places to drink and all kinds of bars. Of course, back in the '70s, a case of beer was a whole $19. Adjusted for inflation, that's about $60. Nowadays, prices for beer and other staples, such as eggs, bread, and milk, fluctuates with the seasons and is determined by whether or not the ice roads are open. Despite the harsh weather, the price of food is lowest in winter, because trucks can deliver the goods less expensively than any other means of transportation.

Maybe the most famous of the Yellowknife bars is the WildCat Café, which was built in the '40s and tucked up on a corner of Old Town. The WildCat is made of logs and legends, which is pretty impressive, since it isn't much bigger than the living room in your house. When I first went up to Yellowknife, it was open all the time. I would go up there and party with my brother-in-law Billy. They used to have dances in there and everything. You'd never think that you'd have a party in that small a space, but they'd have lots of them. When we'd go out partying, there were only the three rules mentioned before: never turn down a free beer, don't waste a hard-on, and don't trust the fart. With those rules under our belts, we'd get drunk and head on down to the WildCat Café. Yeah, dances on Friday night, drinking and fighting and whatever other kinds of trouble you could get into, oh Christ. When a bartender in Yellowknife asked you, "What's your poison?" he wasn't kidding around. Nowadays, the WildCat is just open in the summers to keep the history alive. It's still a nice place to visit, but not like the bad old days.

And as far as bad old days go, well, I've had my share I suppose. When I was twenty-five I was arrested for brawling in the parking lot outside of a bar. I didn't start the fight, but was attempting to finish it when the cops arrived. I was convicted of assault and resisting arrest, and sentenced to four years in the pen. The conviction was reversed on appeal, so I ended up serving seventeen months. During that time I was a model prisoner as far as the guards were concerned, but every week was a fight with some inmate. Many of these people had no purpose in life other than to get themselves into trouble or instigate fights, so I knew that prison wasn't the place for me. I had thought I was indestructible, but whatever volcano they had inside them, it wasn't anything I wanted any part of. Lots of people I knew had thrown away the key on me, but I still had my wife and kids, who stood by me, my dreams ahead of me, and a rubber-tired excavator that could earn me a living in the spring and summer. If I could just make it back to the ice . . .

Eventually, I received a pardon, and my record was expunged, but I still say to this day, and so does my wife, that jail was the best thing that ever happened to me. It made me think about my life. I thought, "Do I want to be in here or do I want to be out there?" I've made a lot of mistakes in my life and even went to jail for one of them, but I also got to where I am now.

S o here you are. You've arrived in Yellowknife. You've had your steak and your beer and you're raring to get on the roads. Not so fast. First you have to take a piss test. Two bands in the result window and you're good to go. One band and you're going home. If it comes back pink, you're pregnant and you're not getting behind the wheel. Pass the piss test and you're cleared for orientation. During orientation, which is taught by the truck companies like RTL Robinson, you'll learn about the roads: what it's like out on the ice, what to expect, what to do and what not to do. It's an open-book course, so not a big deal. You just have to know what they're talking about, especially if you're hauling chemicals, propane, or gas.

A lot of the orientation is about safety, about the speeds you can drive and the conditions you'll be up against. Of course, you learn about good ice and bad, what to look for. The routes and logistics of each are explained. There's load safety and managing both your truck and your hauls in extreme weather. That includes driving tactics and protocol. Tactics are broken into categories: loading and driving. First, you learn how to properly strap down and monitor your loads. Freight carried over a rough road will shift and become unbalanced if you're not careful, so this is important. Driving tactics deal with going on and off ice, hill climbing and descent, speed limits, and dealing with all of the weather conditions you'll face. As far as protocol is concerned, that's about picking up and delivering your loads, dealing with paperwork, and which driver has the right of way, especially in the portages. So everybody is taught when, where, and how they can and should drive. In addition, we learn how dispatch and schedules work, and how traffic is controlled. We learn when we can drive and when we can't, as well as what behavior is expected of us in the camps and what is prohibited on the ice roads. Alcohol, firearms, and drugs are all contraband.

The people who run orientation know that you're there to work, so the information is no-nonsense and right to the point. Equipment, speed limits, and strategies, tactics on hills, convoy procedures, emergency protocol, recovery and rescue operations, and first aid—it's all covered. That said, a lot of the drivers just throw what they've learned out the window as soon as they get in their trucks. That's what I mean by drivers with bad habits. For example, the course teaches you about the dynamics of the wave you'll be pushing when you drive over water, yet you'll still see drivers speeding and blowing out sections of the road. Or you learn never to touch your truck brakes but to use your jack brake instead. (The jack brake is a device inside the engine that shuts down your valves to create drag so your engine will pull up and slow you right down without sending you into a skid.) Of course, on the very first day you'll see drivers sliding across the ice and slamming into snowbanks.

It takes all kinds.

Next, a contract lays out all the rules and regulations of the road. Sign it, or you don't drive. If you're going to haul hazardous materials, you have to inform them, because you'll require a special certification. You'll have to have a criminal record check and your record must be clean. Squeaky-clean. Present your driver's abstract (that's the record of all your accidents and infractions) and your driver's license, too, and you'll be good to go.

Despite orientation, despite all these checks and balances, there are drivers who are unqualified to drive the ice roads. Mainly, they're highway truckers who have never been off pavement. Right away, you can pick them out in orientation. It's the way they talk. They claim to know everything.

"I was born in a truck," one guy said. "Ain't no little patch of ice going to stop me!" No doubt he was accurate about the first part but not the second.

"I'm going to show these Northern boys how we do things down south," another one said.

As if.

Like I say, "Talk is cheap and whiskey costs money." A week into the season some of those same drivers will be getting their courage from a bottle at a bar in Yellowknife, and will be wishing their mothers never met their fathers.

When I see these ice road rookies, I offer advice, and if they don't want to take it, I stay clear of them. I tell them my opinion. I'll say, "You shouldn't be allowed on this road. If I catch you doing anything wrong, I'll report you. If that doesn't work, I'll beat your ass. You even come close to doing something that's going to harm me, and I'll beat your ass." They know I mean business.

Some drivers have no respect for the ice, no regard for other drivers or the customs and traditions of ice road trucking. "Highway maggots" is the nickname for newbie highway drivers from down south whose only intention is to do whatever they can to make a fast buck. I drive the ice roads for the money too. I make no bones about that. But I never lose sight of what's important out there on the roads, and I never lose respect for the ice. That's the difference. These highway maggots often speed and lose control of their rigs and loads, which accounts for many of the head-on collisions and jack-knifing on the portages. Personal experience has shown me the danger these drivers pose. Despite hundreds of runs on the ice over more than two decades, I've always made it through unscathed, although I've had some close calls.

Driving on the ice roads is risky, so you have to have special insurance. It's pretty expensive, as you could imagine: as much as $4,000 per truck for eight weeks of insurance. I have to sign a waiver every year so that the mines (or anyone else, for that matter) aren't liable if I die. I get wrecked, I can't sue. I'm on the ice roads, and I drown? That's my problem. I'm on the ice roads, and I break my arm or leg? That's my problem too. If something happens to me—anything!—well, I'm done. We're all independent contractors, which means that no one who contracts us for a job is liable for anything. I carry my own compensation, so if something happens like that, I'm covered. My trucks are insured, my drivers have to have their own life insurance and everything like that. I guess you could say it's every man for himself.

I like to lessen the odds of something happening, so I make sure to have plenty of emergency supplies and essential spare parts, like alternator belts and hoses for the truck in case I break down, which is guaranteed to happen. The portages are rough on a truck and with temperatures dipping below −60, well, you're going to break down. It will save your hide every time. I don't know about "climate change," but when people outside of the Arctic ask me about global warming, I tell them to come on up and see the icicles hanging from my face. We've had warm winters followed by winters where it was 60 below for weeks at a time. As far as I'm concerned, the cold comes and goes with the decades.

I don't like hanging around town or camp, because you have to listen to the guys who get caught up in the politics of driving. You'll hear them whining, "He promised me this or that." Of course he promised you that, but you didn't have it in writing. "I'll never haul for them again," they say. Well then who's going to buy your kids' clothes and put food on the table? Usually, this is the same type of guy who thinks, "Well, I'm going to screw them—I won't drive my truck next year." So what? They'll just hire somebody else. If you do it for one price, and somebody else will do it cheaper, they'll take the cheaper guy. It's a business, right?

Once you make a deal, you're committed whether you discover it's a bad deal or not. That thinking is going to serve you better in the long run. Just carry on and work, move on to your next deal.

Another reason I don't like camp is the food. It's too easy to waste time eating food that makes you fat and sleepy. Don't get me wrong, they treat us like kings and serve us some of the best meals in the world. Whatever you want, tell them and they will make it right in front of you. Steak and eggs? You got it. We may be thousands of miles from fresh fruit and vegetables, but if you want an apple, they will have one that looks like it just came off the tree. All the cakes, pie, and cookies you could dream of. If I just ate what they prepared in camp—I'd weigh 300 pounds at the end of the nine weeks. Who wants that? I go the other way. I always lose 15 pounds over the course of a season, because I make it a rule not to eat much while I'm on the road. Except breakfast. Have a good, hearty breakfast, like plenty of eggs, bacon, toast, coffee, and juice, and you're good to go for the day. You can skip lunch and even get by on a sandwich in your truck for supper if the circumstances warrant it. If it sounds basic, that's because it is. I know why I'm there and I'm poised like a prize fighter to get at it. For me, there is no greater feeling on earth than clearing orientation, knowing that soon I will be starting my engine and keeping it running nonstop for the next nine weeks.

7

PROMISE AND PERIL

or years, people came north to make their fortunes. In the early days, when a lot of that fortune was in gold, most of the arrivals were prospectors, rough-hewn men staking their claims, who would go out there with anything they could. There was no high-tech equipment back then; they'd just dig a hole and see what they'd come out with. Surprisingly, a lot of the prospectors made good. They'd find gold, then sell their claim and would be set for life. Others didn't hit their strike and went bust. As late as the '70s, you'd see these old prospector and blaster types hanging around Yellowknife looking for a chance to get back out there in the bush. You'd walk into a bar and somebody would be trying to sell you part of a claim. That's gold fever for sure.

For fifty to sixty years, it was gold that everyone was

after. Con was the first successful mine. After that came Negus and then Giant. Giant became wildly successful in the boom that followed the end of World War II and was typical of tales that inspired gold fever. Apparently a Cat skinner had been attempting to move a boulder and haul it to the dump when it was discovered that it was stubbornly embedded in a matrix of bedrock loaded with luminous veins of pure gold. The area around that boulder became Giant Mine. (Personally, I never got gold fever, but then again, when I was digging with my backhoe I was always looking, because you never know . . .) But after that the gold dried up and the mines started closing down. Yellowknife went bust. There's no work if there are no mines, and it doesn't take much to take 20,000 people out of a town when the opportunity goes away. It was back to hardscrabble living for anyone who stayed.

By the late 1980s, it looked like the best days of Yellowknife were behind it. The town received half of its revenue from property taxes, but now housing prices had plunged. A few gold mines were still operating, but the owners claimed that revenue was down. The mines were dank and heavily contaminated with asbestos and toxic arsenic trioxide dust used in the smelting process. A company from out of the area called Royal Oak Mining bought the legendary Giant Mine in 1990, after the price of gold had dropped below the cost of mining. Immediately, operating costs were slashed and production was increased. Complaints were made by the union that the safety of the miners was being sacrificed. If tensions were high, they were about to boil over.

Some workers believed that despite the conditions, despite the fact that union miners were being asked to work harder for less money, these were still the best wages in the Northwest Territories. They desperately wanted to keep working. Others said enough was enough and wanted to strike. Tensions escalated until Yellowknife was cut right down the middle between those who backed the mines or had businesses dependent on the mines, and those who demanded better wages and working conditions. In some cases, rifts came within families. I knew fathers and sons who stopped speaking during this time.

A strike-lockout began in 1992, which lasted eighteen months. The union workers tried to shut down the mines, but the owners brought in replacement or, depending on your point of view, "scab" miners. Pinkertons of Canada (an offshoot of the American security and detective agency founded by Allan Pinkerton in 1850), was also brought in to protect the new workers and the mine. Pinkerton became famous when he foiled a plot to assassinate newly elected president Abraham Lincoln. In gratitude, Lincoln hired Pinkerton agents to be his personal security during the Civil War. The agency continued to grow by offering services ranging from security-guard work to private military contracting. The Pinkerton Agency was even hired to hunt down such outlaws as Jesse James and the Wild Bunch, which included Butch Cassidy and the Sundance Kid. At the height of its success, the Pinkerton National Detective Agency employed more agents than there were members of the standing army of the United States. Such a situation was so unsettling that the state of Ohio outlawed the agency out of concern that Pinkerton could be used as a private militia.

The Pinkerton name has been closely tied to strikebreaking since the volatile labor unrest of the nineteenth century, when Pinkerton agents were hired to infiltrate unions and pro-worker organizations like the Molly Maguires. They were also employed as guards to keep strikers and suspected unionists out of factories. That's one reason why, in response to the arrival of the Pinkerton Agency at Giant Mine, union men from all over Canada descended upon Yellowknife to support the striking miners. The town was full of marches and protests. After several months, some union members crossed the picket line and resumed work. Meanwhile, a small group of striking miners, who called themselves the Cambodian Cowboys, engaged in attempts to sabotage the mine and disrupt operations. At 8:45 a.m. on September 18, 1992, a railcar transporting the replacement workers hit a trip wire 750 feet or fifty-eight stories below the earth's surface, detonating an explosion so powerful that it drove flesh and bone deep into the hard-rock ceiling. The bomb was deliberately set and nine men were killed. In 1995, union miner Roger Warren confessed and was convicted of nine counts of second-degree murder following his confession.

Fifteen years later, Warren remains behind bars (despite recanting his confession), and the wounds inflicted upon families in Yellowknife have yet to heal. Meanwhile, the Northwest Territories Supreme Court found that the union had endorsed much of the sabotage and that Warren had been encouraged to commit the crime by other miners. The court also ruled that Royal Oak had failed to adequately protect the replacement miners and should have known that hiring them would lead to violence. A judge awarded the families of the dead miners $10.7 million in a wrongful-death suit. He ruled that the parties responsible were Royal Oak Mine, Pinkerton of Canada, the miners' union, and the Northwest Territories government. In 2008, the ruling was overturned on appeal.

Against this terrible backdrop, diamonds were discovered.

Chuck Fipke, a down-on-his-luck geologist-turned-prospector, said in the early '90s that the few diamonds people found and the prehistoric volcanoes that dotted the Arctic were related. Everybody thought Fipke, like Denison before him, was crazy. They gave him nicknames like Captain Chaos and Stumpy. If you sat for a cup of coffee with Chuck Fipke, you'd best get ready for the hard sell about diamonds under the ice. I did some exploratory diamond drilling back in the late '70s for one of Chuck's competitors, running a machine that dug holes. I thought the people who hired me had more money than brains. It wasn't a life for me, that's for sure. There was one blaster who worked with me who would drink two bottles of straight whiskey and then drive around Yellowknife tossing lit sticks of dynamite out the truck window. He was driving all over the place, blowing things up. One day, he went to throw a stick out the window of a car, but held on too long and blew off his arm. And I thought I took chances.

Fipke was down to his last pennies when he made the big find at what became known as Diamet, and later Diavik Diamond Mine. That's a pretty common rags-to-riches story for those parts. Everybody hears it and everybody tells it. Funny thing is that we all had the same opportunity to buy shares in Chuck Fipke's diamond mine. At the time, everybody said, "Diamonds in Yellowknife? You're crazy." Even people who bought shares only did it because they liked Chuck and knew he needed the money. Maybe they figured that a harebrained scheme now and again made life interesting. Of course, they're millionaires now, and Chuck is a multimillionaire diamond magnate. Just when Yellowknife was about to go under, Chuck and his diamond strike gave it another chance. People returned in droves, housing prices went up, and the city grew. Yellowknife was saved. That boom that started almost twenty years ago continues today.

Chuck figured it out.

The area around Yellowknife is filled with prehistoric volcanoes. Back before the last Ice Age, the volcanoes had erupted, shooting blasts of hot magma and gas from deep inside the earth up to the surface through vertical tubes called kimberlite pipes. These kimberlite tubes forced their way through the surrounding granite. When the volcanoes cooled and went dormant, the kimberlite pipes were left as calling cards.

Kimberlite pipes are big. The diameter at the surface can

be anything from about a few hundred yards to two-thirds of a mile. Kimberlite is different from surface rock, because it's filled with tightly packed bits of volcanic rock, like buckshot inside a shotgun shell. The story of kimberlite is a good-news-bad-news kind of thing. The good news is that diamonds hitched along for the ride of the erupting magma can be found among the volcanic "buckshot." The bad news is that only one in two hundred kimberlite pipes contains diamonds of gem quality. Still, as Fipke proved, find the right pipes and you're going to make a killing.

Volcanic gravel is black and light. Pick up a piece, rub it, and if you're really lucky, there will be a raw diamond in your hand. But like most things in the Arctic, finding the diamonds isn't the hard part. Getting to them and getting them out of the ground is what takes some doing. Some of the kimberlite tubes are located under lakes that formed in the volcano craters. In places like Snap Lake, they literally dig tunnels below the bottom of the lake to get to the diamonds. Other places are so hard to get to that they had to drop in an owner's claim stake by helicopter.

At mines like Ekati, Diavik, Jericho, and Snap Lake, giant multinational companies such as De Beers, BHP Billiton, Rio Tinto, and Aber mine and process somewhere in the area of 250 tons of ore just to produce one single-carat, gem-quality diamond. It's a lot of work for little pieces of clear rock, but so far it's been worth all the trouble. Some of the highest concentrations of diamonds, not to mention the best quality, come from north of Yellowknife. Since about 1991, they've pulled out more than $3 billion worth of diamonds, and

Canada has gone from not even being on the list to being the third biggest producer in the world.

Mining for diamonds wouldn't make economic sense without the winter roads or the truckers. The mines need fuel, supplies, and machinery, and there's only one viable way in—over the ice roads. In 2007 alone, we delivered 250,000 tons of supplies in just nine weeks. While it's possible to haul up supplies via huge Hercules and Antonov aircrafts, the cost is about eight times greater than going by truck.

I have a very good relationship with the diamond mines. If they have something special to haul that has to get there right away, they ask for me to haul it. They'll phone down to dispatch and say, "Could you get Hugh to bring this up so we know it's going to get here right away?" The mines run 24/7 and are always on a schedule. They want reliable drivers who can keep to that schedule.

I've gone into places where nobody else would go because the roads were tough or dangerous, and I'd haul things no one else would haul. If the mine had a tough, unbalanced, or unsafe load that had to get somewhere the way it was, someone would ask me, "Can you get this load up there?"

"Yeah, no problem," I'd say.

As soon as I turned away I would be thinking, "How the hell am I going to get that load up there?" But I landed the job, which was the important thing. Now it was on my back, not theirs. So I'd take it on, figure it out as I went along, and somehow make it to where I needed to go. The mines never doubted me, but they would be thrilled and sometimes a

My beautiful bride, Dianne, and me on our wedding day back in 1980. I was eighteen and full of piss and vinegar. I'm not eighteen anymore but not much else has changed.

"Little shack on the prairie." The farmhouse I grew up in was only 10 feet wide and not much to look at, but it's pretty much the only thing still standing on the old homestead except for the outhouse. Seven of us lived in that little building. The place is now a buffalo ranch. They still use the steel fences my old man and I put up back in the early eighties to hold our steers.

This picture was taken after one of my luckier days on earth. I had blown a tire at over 100 mph and the truck rolled end over end three times. At one point, I flew out of the window and the truck landed on top, burying me under a foot of mud. Everyone thought I was dead but I was fine except for three ribs that had to be popped back into my spine. It's pretty hard to kill a polar bear.

That's me with my three-year-old granddaughter, Cora Riley, on my Cat. I tried to teach her the tricks of the trade but she didn't like the noise. She likes dancing more so I nicknamed her Freddy G the Dancin' Queen.

Alex Debogorski and me in Anchorage, Alaska, in 2009. Our friendly rivalry has lasted for more than two decades.

At the North Pole with my namesake, the polar bear. He's bigger, but I'm better-looking.

At home in Winfield with the beautiful mountains of British Columbia behind me.
MICHAEL LENT

On a day when it was 48 below zero with more than 4 feet of snow falling, I bagged a 6 × 6 trophy elk by tag-teaming with my son-in-law's father. Most hunters go a lifetime and never get one like this. Twenty minutes later, we bagged a moose, too. It was a hell of a day.

An RTL truck carries a screen deck for a gravel crusher across Prosperous Lake. Tons and tons of ore must be pulverized to find a single diamond.

Black ice is safe ice. As you can see here, the road is long and you can be alone with your thoughts for a lot of it. This is the time when I do my planning for when the season ends.
KEN WORONER, COURTESY OF THE HISTORY CHANNEL

Outside of Inuvik at the intersection of ice roads leading to Langley and Tuktoyaktuk. You can see a giant pingo ice mound in the background. Some of the pingos can be well over 200 feet high and have craters in the middle. The Inuit have used them for spotting and hunting whales for hundreds of years. KEN WORONER, COURTESY OF THE HISTORY CHANNEL

Hauled on a low bed, a rock box from one of the world's biggest rock trucks heads into a blizzard. The box is an entire load all by itself. A rock truck that has been disassembled is so huge that it takes five separate loads to transport over the ice. MICHAEL LENT

Just after a fresh snowfall, a B-Train hauls fuel that is the lifeblood of any operation in the Arctic. KEN WORONER, COURTESY OF THE HISTORY CHANNEL

A water truck crashed through the ice at the start of the season several years ago and was instantly entombed in ice. Luckily, no one was killed, but they left the truck there in the middle of the road as a warning. Turned out to be one of the safest seasons on record. When it was over, they blasted and craned out the truck. KEN WORONER, COURTESY OF THE HISTORY CHANNEL

The Rowland Family Christmas in 2009. Left to right from the back row is: Aunt Susy in red; Paul, my brother-in-law in black; my mother-in-law, Betty Lou; my oldest daughter, Karly, with her hubby, Jay; youngest daughter, Candace, and her hubby, CJ. Front row: my wife, Dianne, in the Santa hat; Leanne, Dianne's sister and Paul's wife; me; my middle daughter, Chandra-Jo, and her hubby, Jesse, who are the parents of my two grandchildren; three-year-old grandson, Dutch Bronson, who everyone calls "Little Hugh" (on Leanne's lap), and my five-year-old granddaughter, Cora Riley. She's on her dad's knee.

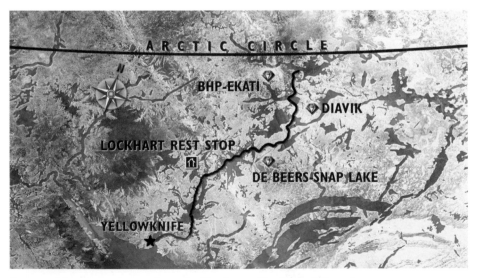

A map of the winter ice roads in the Northwest Territory of Canada
© 2009 AETN/PHOTO CREDIT: ORIGINAL PRODUCTIONS

little relieved to see my truck pulling up. There might have been a story or two along the way, but I saved them until after I made the delivery. The manager would show his appreciation with a gravy load going back, so that I would make double for the run. It's a system of "Scratch my back, and I'll scratch yours." We have a good rapport and get along real well.

I made deliveries on the ice roads when the diamond mines first opened. Beginning in 1994, in a matter of three short years, diamonds in the Arctic had gone from being a fool's errand to being a rumor to being a reality. There were a total of forty runs on the ice that first winter. That number more than quadrupled to one hundred seventy-five in the second season, then leaped to four hundred in year three. Four hundred loads was beyond belief. Ice road trucking had always been a part-time job to tide you over in the dead of winter. Now here was a full-time opportunity. Of course, people in town talked about the danger of driving on the ice. In the gold-mine days rarely had so many runs been made with such heavy weight. Meanwhile, the new roads built to service the diamond mines were terrible. Building them and measuring the ice was rudimentary at best.

The drivers were all rookies with not the slightest clue how to drive, and there was no security to monitor safety and establish protocol. Sometimes you had two trucks coming into a narrow space from opposite directions and both refused to give way. It was like the Wild West. That said, drivers were well compensated for the risk. Work has always been catch-as-catch-can in the Arctic. It was a tall order to stay employed for an entire twelve months. With the ice roads, you could set a little money aside for lean times or to invest in your future. When a few drivers had completed runs that first winter, I listened to the stories of promise and peril. I decided I didn't mind getting my share of both. I had arrived in Yellowknife with little more than the clothes on my back and there was no chance at an opportunity that I wasn't prepared to take. Years later, people would say that I was lucky to be in the right place at the right time, but to me, that's just what happens when you work hard and take a chance. My philosophy has always been, You can't always drive on the road somebody else made. Sometimes you have to make your own way.

I had a family, like everybody else, so I wasn't going to risk my neck for nothing. However, while others called the ice roads Russian roulette and the height of insanity, I had at last found something that made perfect sense to me. I had always battled and defied the odds just to survive. Now someone wanted to pay me a lot of money for what I had been doing all along. I wasn't afraid as far as risk was concerned, because the rougher things got, the more sure of myself I became. If your life is about shouldering a load, then who's better than you? What's better than your own shoulders? On the ice, all the fractures of life are made whole. I also remembered that back in 1978, RTL had transported a 190,000-pound generator over the ice from Yellowknife to Port Radium on Great Bear Lake, more than 300 miles away. That was good enough insurance for me.

I don't think about freezing to death or falling through the ice or any of that other stuff. If I did, I wouldn't be able to do what I do. My very first truck, that Western Star, barely had heat. Compared to the trucks of today, she was a beast.

I never had my own trucks in the early years. I'd just drive them for somebody else. Most of the company trucks I drove were rust-bucket castoffs that no one took the time to maintain. I didn't buy my own rigs until there were enough loads, which meant money to be made. Back then, there was no such thing as security or speed limits on the ice roads. Drivers were always going off the roads. They'd crash into a snowbank, get pulled out, and away they'd go. When the trucks broke down, and they always did, somebody would come from the company and pick them up. *That's* when they would get them winter-ready. The only time a truck got any sort of maintenance is when it broke down. It was a hell of a system.

Some of the old trucks had no insulation. You'd be in a snowstorm, but you couldn't defrost the windows. If you did, you'd need wipers, and half of the trucks didn't have them. So you'd clean the windows one time, when you first started out, and never turn your heater on the windows. The snow would just hit and blow off the cold glass.

If you did happen to have a real heater, which was rare, the trick was to keep it going on the floor and away from the windows. Have a heater too close to the windows and they'd fog up and you wouldn't be able to see a thing. Most trucks had an auxiliary box heater in the middle of the truck that was supposed to heat the whole cab. It didn't work very well, though. You'd be driving in a snowstorm and look down at your feet to see drifts as high as your boots across the floor.

Promise and Peril

If you put your water jug down, it would be frozen solid when you picked it up again. The trucks were drafty, too. If the wind was coming hard on one side, you would have to stuff your sleeping bag over your legs to prevent them from freezing. Otherwise, your leg would freeze from your hip to your feet. Frost on the walls would be half an inch thick. You could carve your name in it. In those old garbage trucks that we had, you always wore every bit of gear you had. No heat and no place to sleep. You'd be bundled like an Eskimo on the hunt, and if you had any luck at all, you had a tiny peephole out the front window to look through.

The roads were a lot different then. Most ice roads were only wide enough for one truck to drive on. If you came to a portage, you were supposed to get on your CB and say, "Northbound, portage 15." That meant you were carrying a load. "Southbound, portage 15" meant you had already delivered your load and were running empty. But the CB signals didn't go far, and certainly not over a hill. Consequently, trucks would be coming from different directions, unaware of each other and unable to stop. The road wouldn't be wide enough for them to pass each other, so they'd be smashing mirrors all the way through. If you went off the road, there was no way to pull you out. You might be stuck there for a day.

On those first hauls, we were all making it up as we went along: the diamond companies, the road builders, the freight yard, the truck companies, the dispatchers, and the drivers. All of us. This was a time before Orientation. A time before Security and ground radar. Nobody knew to measure ice thickness. You were simply told that the ice was fine, and off you went on a wing and a prayer. Trucks would be loaded without regard to weight, and we drove without regard to following distance. It was common to see a clogger (a slow-moving, overly cautious driver or truck carrying an oversize load that clogged up the flow of traffic) followed by three or four tailgaters. No one stopped to think that you might be stressing a single chunk of ice with 300,000 to 400,000 pounds of weight. It's a miracle we weren't all killed. My driving strategy was simple: Load up, get in, sit down, start driving, hold on. I forget the exact memory of that first haul except that I rocked and rolled my way through it. It was a crazy, dangerous carnival ride that I was thrilled as hell to be on.

It was something all right, driving up and knowing that diamonds were being mined just a little ways from where you parked your truck. Sometimes you'd see little glints right there on the ground in the parking lot. Tell me that's not tempting. But the mines were strict about security. They had spotters with binoculars who would watch you as soon as you drove up to the mine. Most of the drivers saw those little glints, but those who couldn't resist them, those of us who actually bent down to pick them up, were escorted from the premises right away and weren't allowed to make more deliveries. That was it. You were persona non grata. No picking anything up. No putting anything in your pockets. That was the rule. Later on, they wouldn't even let you out of your truck. Employees from the mines would do the loading and unloading while you waited in your cab. Sometimes that could take as long as two hours. Plenty of time for a nap.

My sister Terry works at one of the mines. She is very, very quiet and her job at the mines suits her just fine. Terry was shy when she was young, and she still is. Yellowknife is the right place for a person like that. She moved up there in '77 and never left. You can count on one hand the number of times she's come down south in the past thirty-odd years. Terry works as a sorter, and every single day she sorts out and fills a container the size of a coffee can with diamonds. As you might guess, the process is a carefully guarded trade secret; however, I can tell you that there are two major steps involved in sorting. First, all those tons of ore that a mining operation yields by blasting and digging have to be sifted, so that the diamonds are separated from the other materials. Next, the judgment of trained and skilled individuals is required to sort gem-quality stones from industrial-grade stones.

The mechanical sorting process relies mainly on cones and cyclones to sift out the high density of diamonds. Diamond-bearing concentrate is mixed with a fluid with a density close to that of diamonds. The separation occurs by swirling the mixture at low and high velocities in cones and cyclones, respectively. Cyclones are just about 100 percent efficient at separating diamonds and similar dense minerals from the original ore. With 99 percent of the waste in the ore removed, an X-ray separator may catch anything that the cones and cyclones might have missed.

Manual sorting is the next step. Skilled individuals like my sister Terry sort the recovered diamonds by examining each piece through a jeweler's loupe. Rough diamonds can be sorted into three different categories. First, there's gem quality. That's about the clarity, size, shape, and color they always tell you to look for in the stores. Only about 20 percent of all rough diamonds are good enough for jewelry. Industrial quality counts for the remaining 80 percent of good stones. These industrial diamonds, while of good quality, are reserved for industrial use, such as crushing-boart or boart. The boart can be found in dozens of products for the construction industry, including diamond blades, diamond core bits, diamond wire, wall saws, flat saws, core drills, masonry saws, tile saws, power cutters, and gang saw blades. Stones with the worst diamond quality are crushed to be used as diamond dust, which, in turn, is used to cut and polish gem-quality diamonds.

After the diamonds are sorted by Terry and her colleagues, they go through the marking and cutting process. The mines use lasers to etch a little polar bear and a serial number onto the side of the diamond along the girdle that you can only see with a microscope or a special light. That's how you know these are the real Arctic diamonds and not blood diamonds from war zones in Africa used to buy guns and arm insurgents or anything like that. It's a lot of work for a little rock that looks to me like a piece of glass.

Terry has a house in town, 190 miles away, but she often lives in a dorm at the mine. The dorms are quite something, where they have everything you'd ever want for the 750 employees. Besides cafeterias and stores, there are movie theaters, game rooms, fitness centers, lounges, libraries, and mail centers. There's even a bowling alley. Sometimes Terry doesn't go home for a week or more, especially when the weather is bad and she can't get out. The pay is good—I guess they don't want their employees to feel hard-done-by or resentful—even so, she has to be X-rayed and strip-searched every day. Terry works alone inside of a vault, where every move she makes is watched by a bunch of cameras and is recorded. Her unit sends those tapes out to another part of the company, where they're watched again, analyzed, and catalogued. All the eyes on you were a little tough to deal with at first, but Terry says you get used to it, and that good pay makes up for it. At this point, she doesn't even think about it anymore.

There are lots of other things in those kimberlite pipes, including sapphires, rubies, garnets, and gold. However, anything that's not a diamond goes back on the scrap pile. All of it. The companies are only there for diamonds, and it's too much trouble to try to process anything else. Some of the mines allow the public to come in now and again to haul away a truckload of ore from the slag pile. I suppose you might find some gems and gold in there if you're patient and know what to look for. After Terry had been with the company for a while, they gave her a diamond as a show of appreciation. Out of the thousands that have passed through her hands worth tens of millions of dollars, that's the only one she cares to own.

8

WORKING FOR A POLAR BEAR

've got a pretty good life—a beautiful family, my own house, my own business. It wasn't always that way. The house I grew up in had electricity but no running water or indoor plumbing. We caught rainwater off the back of the house in a big galvanized metal tub and boiled the water to use for cooking and everything else. Bath day was once a week.

Mom, Dad, and my sisters slept in one room, and I had a bed out beside the deep freeze and the woodstove. The house sat on a wood foundation and the floors were slanted. Severely slanted. You could drop a golf ball at one end and it would build up a head of steam by the time it raced into the area we called my bedroom. When you live like that, no one has to tell you you're poor. You wake up and you go to bed knowing it.

I played hooky a lot, but when I did go to school I was the class clown. I was always in trouble for pranks but still managed to play all kinds of sports, including basketball, volleyball, wrestling, and boxing. My old man hated the fact that I played sports, so I'd have to walk or find my way home from a competition. Despite my antics, school came naturally to me. If you maintained at least an 85 average, you didn't have to take the final exams. I was always in trouble, but I never had to take final exams. Years later, when I had kids of my own—three girls—I was able to help them with their trig homework in the eleventh or twelfth grade. Not bad for a dropout, eh?

By the seventh grade, I was getting kicked out all the time. That was just fine with my dad. He hadn't gone past the seventh grade and preferred that I work the farm with him. Mom always said that I was smart enough to be a doctor or a lawyer, or whatever else I wanted, but I was too wild and liked to be outside. I never gave those other things a thought.

At the age of fifteen, they threw me out of school for good. That was all right with me. I'd been working since I was a kid and was ready to get at her. A few years before, during the summer when I was eleven, I had gone to work for a road construction crew. They paid me $1.50 an hour to shovel and rake the tar. I was laboring on the road in the hot sun, but when I got that first paycheck, I thought to myself, "This is the answer." The Scottish have a saying, "A man is a lion in his own cause," and that summer I worked twice as hard as I ever had before.

So, from a young age I knew how the world worked and what I had to do to get my share. I shoveled and raked from sunup to sundown all summer, then took all the money I earned and bought cows. Once I had that going, I wanted to get some steers, but my father said, "I'm tapped out and can't get any more money. Maybe you can go in and get a loan from the bank. I'll go with you and see what happens," My father knew that I already had a better business sense than he did, so I did all of the talking and walked out with a $30,000 loan that my father co-signed using the farm as collateral. Fourteen months later, I sold the steers at market, paid off the loan and put $12,000 in my pocket. By then, I was all of twelve years old and used the money to buy pigs and more cows. And a brand-new truck.

From that point on, at any given time, we had a hundred head of cattle, five hundred to fifteen hundred chickens and fifty sows. I used to get up in the morning at 5:00 and go out and feed all the livestock, then change my clothes and go to school. It was the same drill when I came home at night. I was good at farming but it was backbreaking work with low rates of return on your investment. My hat is off to anyone that can make a go of it.

From those early days I learned, "Get what you can and keep what you have; that's the way to get rich."

I've done a lot of crazy things my whole life, on and off the ice, from bull riding to brawling. I take lots of risks and the tougher the job, the better I like it. Desk jobs aren't for me, that's for sure. But there are risks, like the first time I went into the water nearly twenty years ago. I was trying to cross a frozen river while driving a D-7 Cat. The running water in rivers keeps the ice thin and makes them particularly dangerous and unstable, more so than lakes. This one was the Wild Hay River out in the Rockies. That day, the water was running across the top in places. That's a bad sign. My job was to plow the road so everybody else could come across. No one liked the look of the ice, and everyone thought I was crazy, but I said, "I'll go across. If it goes down, I'll jump." I've never refused a challenge. Besides, the temperature was dropping, which I figured was a big plus in my favor. Behind me were two more Cats with drivers waiting to see what would happen, and then a line of trucks ready to go out onto the ice. You can bet your ass they were all taking bets.

At first, it was smooth sailing. I was moving along and the ice held me up. All of a sudden, I heard a loud rumble, like thunder, and a sharp cracking sound. Before I could react, there was another loud crack that echoed across the water, and then the Cat busted right down through the ice. It was by blind chance that I still had my blade up. The coldest water in the world came whooshing up over the Cat tracks, right across the running boards, and swirled around my feet. I gave a yell and was scared shitless, ready to bail. Lucky for me, the top layer was flood ice. When water runs over the top of ice and the temperature drops quickly, you get a superficial top layer of flood ice that can form like a scab on a wound. Trapped between the flood ice and the true ice surface of the river can be a layer of water that will give you a sandwich, with a thin top of ice, a middle of water, and a bottom of ice that began forming in November but is now starting to disintegrate.

The Cat was submerged about four feet down but resting

on the lower ice underneath. The only thing I heard was the run of the water. Somehow the bottom ice held. It was so cold that new ice started forming around the Cat right away. You could look down and see it crystallizing right before your eyes. In no time at all, it was frozen in place.

When all the adrenaline waves slowed down and I was able to catch my breath, I climbed down slowly and carefully, no worse for wear, with nothing more than wet boots that were already stiffening up in the cold. Across the ice, I could hear the other Cat drivers hollering at me. I waved them off and, after assessing the situation and realizing what had happened, I climbed back up on the Cat. I backed up the vehicle to the edge of the ice where I fell through. I kept listening to the ice the whole time, but it was holding steady.

Tail between my legs, I walked back across the ice to rejoin my group and take whatever shit they were going to dish out. After explaining my predicament, another driver said he was willing to test his luck too, in order to get me out of there. The other Cat followed me onto the ice to the spot where I went in. The driver hooked his winch line to my machine. I climbed aboard my Cat, put it in gear. The winch sucked me up as I backed up from the edge. I walked the Cat right out of there.

That night, we hoisted more than a few beers to toast my good fortune, then had a brawl about who was the best Cat driver. In the morning, we were all the best of friends again. We figured the river would freeze up enough for us to cross if we just gave it a couple more days. In the meantime, we built some pipeline ice bridges and then a road around my hole.

So that was my first time going into the drink. It certainly wasn't my last. Talk about more guts than brains. In the morning, we attached a 100-foot towline to the Cat and dragged it out.

Driving on ice may be dangerous, but it's not glamorous. Not to me, anyway. Sometimes you get drivers who are used to eight-hour days who'll want to try it on the ice roads. Good luck with that. The ice roads are never an eight-hour day. In fact, that first stop takes more than eight hours all by itself, just to get to De Beers and Snap Lake about 140 miles north of Yellowknife. The companies that hire us want the wheels to keep turning, the more runs the better. They're operating 24/7 and they're paying good money for good drivers. They don't want anyone behind the wheel fool enough to think he can get away with an eight-hour day.

De Beers alone has 560 employees and an automated process plant capable of handling 3,150 tons of ore each day. They also have on-site water-and-sewer treatment plants, a utilities building to power the entire operation, and an airstrip capable of landing 737 jets and Hercules C-130 transport planes. The cost of constructing and operating the mine is well over $1 billion. With an operation that big, resupply via the ice roads is vital.

I don't take myself too seriously, but I sure am serious about my job. That's something I expect of the people who work for me too. Lucky for me, I get to pick from some of the best. Seems like people from all over the world want to run the ice roads with me. One guy showed up at my doorstep all the way from Ireland! He just showed up. He had seen the show and told his wife that he wanted to go to British Columbia for vacation. I was flattered by the interest from so far away but explained there were a lot of steps, like work visas that had to be obtained, before I could even consider hiring him. Other people have called me, sometimes in the dead of night, from places like the United Kingdom, Australia, Germany, and the United States. They've seen me on the TV show, and want to run with the Polar Bear. The ice isn't a place for dreamers, and quickly becomes a polar prison, so I've never hired any of them, but I understand why they heed the call to adventure.

I hire three drivers every season, and I ask them each three questions.

"Are you okay working twenty-four hours a day, seven days a week?" That first question gets rid of a lot of them. If they seem unsure, I'll tell them that a couple of seasons ago, two drivers even died in their trucks. It happens. The trucks were parked and they died from heart attacks, poor bastards. Anyway, telling them that sure separates the men from the boys.

The second question is, "What does your wife think of this?" If a guy answers, "Well, I'm just trying to talk her into it," I'll shake my head no. "You're not working for me," I'll tell him. "No ifs, ands, or buts." If a guy has to ask his wife if he can go, then he's not coming.

My last question is a simple "Why do you want to drive the ice roads?" Believe it or not, some guys will answer "Just to say I've done it," as if the ice roads are some kind of adventure, something to impress their neighbors or their drinking buddies. I won't give the time of day to guys like that. If all you want to do is to say you've done it, go on . . . say you've done it and save

Working for a Polar Bear

us both a lot of trouble. In fact, say what you want, but you're not going to make it and you're not coming with me.

If, on the other hand, a guy tells me he needs the money, he's staying. The ones who need the money are the ones who are going to stay and stick it out. The guys who sacrificed something from here to go up there—well, I know they'll stay, that's for sure. Drivers make all sorts of sacrifices to ride the ice roads. They might be leaving their wife and kids behind. That's tough. I know that firsthand. Or they might have taken a leave of absence from their regular job. There's always a chance, when they do, that their old job won't be waiting for them, but they may not think they have any other option. People make tough choices when they have to. They make sacrifices today so that things will be better for them and their families tomorrow. I respect that.

It's important for me to know why a driver wants to drive the ice roads, because that will tell me a lot about his commitment. Up there on the ice, at 30 below, commitment counts for a lot. Some drivers have a story about how they want to better themselves. Maybe they want to start their own business. Well, with thirty grand in their jeans, they can start their own business, right? For 10 percent or even 25 percent down, they could go to the bank with thirty grand and borrow $100,000 to start a business, and do something they always wanted to. I've known guys who have taken their ice road money and bought crazy things like float planes. These are guys who don't even have a pilot's license but now they have their very own airplane. Other guys buy toys like snowmobiles, motorcycles, or ATVs. Some are sensible and put a down payment on a house. The ice roads are a good place to better your means. That's how I think. Of course, a lot of guys just want the extra money, and will carry on with their lives in pretty much the same way when the season is over. I understand that, too.

You've got to have sticking power if you want to work for me. And I never ask anybody to do what I won't do, that's for sure. Twenty-five loads, about two-thirds of my haul, is what I ask. Most drivers can get more than that if they stick it out for the season, so it's a reasonable goal. I tell my drivers that on the ice roads they can work as hard as they want. I'll take them up the road. They can travel with me as long as they want, but when they get tired and it's time for them to sleep, then they're on their own. I show my drivers what to do, and then I say, "It's up to you. You can make as much money as you want here, so get at her."

And then I let them go.

Before the season starts, I'll give every driver I hire five grand. A lot of guys have never had that kind of money in their hand before, so when they get that lump sum, they know I mean business. If they're working a nine-to-five job, they're probably only clearing $2,000 to $2,500 a month. So I give them five grand—that's two months' wages right there. "Give it to your wife so she can keep things going while you're gone," I'll tell them. "Now you're going to go up here and make $30,000." That's half what I can make in a season, but most have never seen that kind of money.

Work for me, and I'll set it up so that all you have to worry about is driving, but I tell every driver that he'd better plan on finishing the season. If he doesn't, then he'll be finding his own way home. I never beat around the bush with the

Working for a Polar Bear

drivers who work for me. Business is business and pleasure is pleasure. If you can't do it, I'll get someone who can.

Not many drivers last more than a season or two. It's a big commitment that most can't stick with longer than that. Matter of fact, few of the original diamond-road drivers that came up with me in the '90s are still around. Most cashed it in a long time ago. A few will reappear to drive on the ice for a season when they need some quick cash. Sometimes we'll meet on the road or in the camp and they'll be shocked to learn that I'm still here, that I never went away.

"Too many hits to the head," I'll say. "I'm like a pit bull with a pot roast."

Truth is, I've been a hunter my whole life. I'm at my best when I'm on the move. The ice roads have become a white whale that I've pursued and bested again and again. If success has meant eating and sleeping less than others, so be it. No matter what anybody else thinks or whose feelings I may hurt, I'll work alone and often. When others run away from the ice, I'll go toward it. Most are satisfied to go for a season, take their money, and say that they've done it. But for me, the ice is always calling. The longer I'm away, the more I itch to hunt that white whale.

Show me a guy who has never failed and I will show you a guy who never put anything on the line. To me, if you're giving it your all, then falling short is just part of the game. It all depends on how you bounce back. One thing I have no place for is doubt or fear.

If I did, I couldn't do what I do. In my line of work, instinct is everything and a split second of hesitation can get you killed. Throw yourself into the situation and figure it out as you go along. There's not much you can accomplish in life if you don't start by believing in yourself. Trust me on that.

So you've got that first week under your belt and are heading into the second. In that second week of the season, you might expect the ice to be between 26 and 30 inches thick. At 28 inches, you can haul loads that will weigh up to 31 tons.

Playtime for the newbies is over. It's time to haul ice and turn and burn tonnage.

The roads are still being broken in, but people are running night and day. A driver who spins out on a portage will be stuck like a mastodon in a tar pit. Unable to gain any momentum or traction, that truck ain't going anywhere and will require a tow out. Traffic will back up for hours. That will cost drivers, the freight companies, and the diamond mines tens of thousands of dollars per hour. I will do just about anything to keep going. I've blown methyl hydrate into a brake line to free up an ice blockage. WITH MY OWN LIPS. Talk about the kiss of death. That stuff is straight poison. Swallow any of it and you're dead. I've risked it lots of times because you only have a few minutes to dissolve the blockage before you have bigger problems, like brakes frozen solid. Like I said, hesitation is what will kill you. So you just cross your nuts and hope for the best.

The ice road record for deliveries out of Yellowknife is forty-five loads in sixty days. Farther north, up in Inuvik, sixty-eight hauls in a season is tops. I own both records. If you consider that each round trip requires a minimum of eighteen hours, mechanical breakdowns are a fact of life, and storms so severe that you can't see past the end of your hood are a three-times-a-month occurrence, then you have a sense of not only what our schedules are like but also what it takes to be top dog.

Of course, temperature also factors into how easy those loads will be to move. Rookie drivers spend their first week freezing their asses off and cursing the Arctic air. To them, cold is cold. It isn't. True, if you're caught out in weather of 35 degrees below zero or colder, freezing to death is inevitable. That said, there's a big difference between 40 below and 60 below. If any of those newbies make it to a second week, they learn to pay attention to the thermometer. I keep an eye on the temps too, but it's your nose that lets you know just how cold it is first. The crispness of the air as you breathe tells you everything.

On a "warm" day, you can still move around pretty well. Thirty below doesn't faze me much because I'm active. I hardly even notice it. When you start talking about 10 below, then it's okay to have your lighter gear. I might not even wear my rabbit-fur hat. A ball cap is enough. Of course, you still have to be careful. Sometimes I'll be working so hard strapping loads that I'll start sweating. Once you stop moving, all that moisture quickly turns to ice. Once you have that situation, your muscles can tighten and lock up. Flexing your arms or bending your knees will be like trying to bend granite. To prevent this, I'll remove my hat or gloves, which allows heat to escape quickly and keeps my temperature constant.

On the very coldest days, the sky is the color of lead in a pencil. The sun struggles just to make an appearance. It looks all washed out and faraway. You look around to see vapor and steam coming off every living thing in great big, engulfing clouds. The trucks in the yard are huffing exhaust that looks like a locomotive's steam stack. Even your footsteps leave little ghost trails of steaming smoke as you crunch along. At 60 below and beyond—nearly 100 degrees below the freezing point—your fingers and toes start to sting within about sixty seconds. No matter how good your gear is, the cold will relentlessly attack your body and you will just have to work through the pain. Breathe out of your mouth for too long and your tongue can freeze to your mouth. Of course, it's even easier for your nostrils to freeze together, but you can loosen things up by putting a glove-warmed hand on your nose. I double-time it when the weather is really harsh because your skin and lungs can't stand up to that kind of cold for very long, so you've got to hustle. That's not easy, because your body wants to creep along and make little movements or not move at all, but I say to myself, "Get going. Keep moving." If you don't want the ice to be your final resting place, you've got to keep moving.

At −40 you can still jump out onto the running board of your moving truck to take a piss. At 60 below it's a big operation. You have to put on all of your gear and be ready to rush out and rush back in. Your urine will be frozen before it hits the ground. I warn all of my drivers, "Shake her once instead of three times, boys and girls, and then haul ass to get back in before your 'equipment' freezes to your hand." That's a hell of a way to drive and tough to explain while you're waiting for things to thaw out.

When it's that cold, you have to be careful what you touch with bare skin, especially metal. In the old days of floor heaters that barely worked, I'd hunker down for the night, bundled up in my sleeping bag, only to wake with my nose fused to the bag, glued by the moisture in my breath. Pulling away too quickly would cause the skin to tear like paper.

Of course, temperature isn't the only indicator of cold. Quiet air is preferable to a sharp wind that feels like a straight razor slashing your face. When the wind whips and blows 40-below-zero air, no gear can stand up to it for more than a few minutes. You might as well be wearing nothing but your birthday suit. Back in 1991, the winds were so fierce that we had to hunker down and wait out the storm. We call that "a blow." There were about 140 trucks stranded together for two days. My truck rocked back and forth nonstop until so much snow piled up beneath the wheels, the entire loaded truck was raised 18 inches off the ground. I was pulling a B-train double load weighing at least forty tons of cement, but it didn't matter.

Of course, the weather is tough on the trucks themselves, too. I remember one time it was about 68 below and we were on some pretty rough roads. I felt my load starting to buck. The metal springs that held the rear end of my truck in place were snapping like toothpicks. I had to pull over. All along the road, people were breaking springs, breaking their fifth wheels, and breaking their front axles clean off. You didn't know what was going to snap off next. It was terrible.

If you're lucky, everything will be humming along by week three. The ice will thicken and the loads will get heavier, which means you'll put even more money into your pocket with every haul. Still, it's got to be said that no two seasons are alike. That's one thing I've learned over the years, that's for sure. In the old days, the loads were few and the roads were rough. Each year, the roads got better and the loads heavier. Plus, there were more of them. Sometimes we'd have storms and cold weather lasting weeks. Other times, the winter would be unseasonably mild. The roads would open late and shut down early.

Driving up the McKenzie Delta up on the Beaufort Sea, now that was different. There was no land to cross. We were on ice the whole time, dealing with high and low tides. The tides were coming in and going out, so now we were dealing with weak and strong ice every day. You learn to watch the full moons on a drive like that, because a full moon is a lot closer and pulls harder on the tides and raises the water levels. Higher water weakens the ice, just thins it right out. That's a challenge.

The main thing to realize is that the ice is different every single day. Take Dalton Highway, which is Alaska Route 11. Now, there's a drive. The Dalton is a 414-mile road over land that I'd been hearing about since I was a kid. It's mainly a truck road, and it runs alongside the Alaskan Pipeline. It's a pretty rough road, so the road crews actually spray the roads down with water that turns to ice upon contact with the frigid air. This ice can be scraped to form a rough, durable surface or mixed with sand to create good traction.

In Alaska, there are high mountain passes where you can tip your rig, or worse. A tired or distracted driver can go right off a cliff. The Dalton Highway, aka the Haul Road, may not see as much traffic as Yellowknife (six thousand loads in twelve weeks), but even on the best days, it's no joke. One of the deadliest pieces of road in the world, the desolation of the place and the wind shears wear you right down. Everything is white on white. The roads are narrow and the edge is tight. Trucks pass each other within a foot in places. Miscalculate and you'll trade mirrors. The second you lose focus is the second you go off those steep roads. Turn your head for a second at the wrong time, and when you look back, you're off the road and going over a 500-foot drop. Some sections drop like roller coasters. When the road is frozen with a light glaze of ice, you can find yourself in a situation where the load in your trailer can start pushing you. It feels like having someone heavy on your back as you're trying to make your way down a flight of stairs. If you don't keep your line straight, the trailer can pick up speed and start to pass you. Now the tail is wagging the dog and you've got big trouble. With so many things that can go wrong, hundreds have lost their lives since the Dalton was opened in 1974. Those deaths are never far from your mind, especially when you see the dozens of steel crosses, painted white, lining the road to mark recent fatalities.

Wind shears, falling rocks, and giant potholes are just part of what you can expect. Some of the potholes are the size of small craters and will tear up your suspension and shocks. Mechanics over at the Carlile Yard Garage in Fairbanks routinely work from 6:30 in the morning to 2:30 the next morning to keep the trucks going. The rocks come down from high up on the mountain. They are particularly dangerous when they land on the road. A passing eighteen-wheeler can kick one up the size of a baseball and send it whizzing at your windshield at 50 miles an hour. You'll never see it until it shatters the window right in front of you. The consequences can be deadly. Unlike the ice roads of Yellowknife, small passenger vehicles are allowed on the Dalton, which adds to the list of distractions. Breakdowns are common, yet roadside assistance and repair shops are nonexistent. The Dalton runs right through grizzly country, which is why something like 90 percent of the population carries handguns. Don't even think about driving here without four-wheel drive, a truck or CB radio, extra food, fuel, belts, tires, flares, and warm clothes.

The most northern truck stop in the world is in Coldfoot. They've recorded temperatures as low as −82 (hence the name). It's one of the few places where you can get a hot meal on the entire Dalton Highway.

There are no cliffs in Yellowknife, so tired drivers start running off roads and crashing into snowbanks. You pull them out and they go down the road a bit and they plow into another snowbank. The ice is thickest in the middle of the road and thinner on the sides. If you go through a snowbank, technically you aren't even on the road anymore. Thickness of the ice can go from 40 inches right down to 22. Ice that thin will not sustain a 100,000-pound load for very long. You have to get out of there quick. When people get themselves in a situation, I'll pull them out but tell them, "Hey, listen, pal. Better pull it over on the next portage and have yourself a nap."

No matter where you are in the Arctic, drivers, too, have their own prep to do. We have to spray-paint an orange or yellow spot on our tires so that we can look back and make sure they're still turning and not locked up. At these temperatures, metal fuses to metal and brake pads lock onto the wheels, causing them to stop turning. Believe it or not, you can drive for miles on a frozen tire that isn't rotating—the rubber just glides along on the ice. You'll go to slow down for a portage and that's when you'll discover that your brakes and wheels are frozen into a single unit. If you're lucky, there'll be a snow-bank and someone will happen along to pull you out. If you're not lucky . . . there will be a tree or oncoming truck with your name on it. My brake pads snapped right off driving in the extreme cold once. It was 62 below. I ran over a gaping crack in the ice and immediately heard a huge BANG coming from the wheel. The metal that made up one of my zed or Z springs had become so porous in the cold that it shattered like glass when I hit the crack. I crawled the truck to the nearest portage and disconnected the load from my truck. I called my driver Rick Yemm on the radio. He was just finishing a delivery, so I told him to come get my load and deliver it for me. I was going to try to limp back to town. He thought I was a little crazy, because Yellowknife was 140 miles away, but Rick had come to expect nothing less from me. As long as I went slow and sure and watched my speed and the gear I was in, I figured I would be just fine. Indeed, that turned out to be the case.

There are only three towns over the whole 414 miles of the

Dalton: Coldfoot, Wiseman, and Deadhorse. You can hardly call Coldfoot and Wiseman towns, though. Not with just fifteen or twenty people living there. At least Coldfoot has a truck stop. The Dalton gets a fair amount of truck traffic, but if you have a breakdown out there, you're pretty much screwed. The grades are steep, as much as 12 percent. Going down is like a roller coaster. Of course, the load will be pushing your truck pretty hard and if you're not careful, you'll jackknife. The trick is to speed up so you'll be steady as she goes. And going up, well, you can put on the chains. You better grab a gear you're comfortable with and make sure you don't give her too much power. A lot of guys will hit her hard and then spin out. Once you get stuck, there's no way to make it up without getting towed.

I wouldn't take a brand-new truck on the ice roads, but many do. If trucking is their life and their whole livelihood, then I guess they don't have another choice. Trucks suffer from the cold just as intensely as us drivers. When I see somebody come up north with a brand-new truck, it makes me sick to my stomach. I think, "Oh, that's a shame!" Trucks have the snot beaten out of them on the winter roads. Once you start your engine, it will stay on for the rest of the season. If you shut it down, there's a good chance your truck might not start again. If that happens in the wrong place and at the wrong time, you could freeze to death. So a truck will run for 1,600 to 1,700 hours straight once it arrives in Yellowknife. The engine never shuts off and the truck is always working. The hours, the roads, and the weather conditions combine to shorten a truck's life considerably. Of course, when it's that cold, everything turns brittle.

I don't truck all year round. I just truck up there during the ice season, so I don't have to make that hard choice. All of my trucks are bought at an auction. I look for reliable models with just a few years on them, which have been gently used. I own four rigs that I run during the ice road season: three International Eagles and one Western Star. The Internationals have 550 horsepower engines, and the Western Star has 575 horses. I like the Internationals best, because they can take whatever I can dish out and will still drive like a Cadillac. Plus, they're easy to fix and cheap for parts. All my trucks have four-way lockups, so you don't spin out and have to chain so much.

My trucks are easily identifiable up in Yellowknife. They have my company logo on the door: R & R Hoe Services. That's my excavation company back down south in Winfield. That's where I live and keep my trucks during the off-season. In Winfield, I can work on the trucks and make sure they're ready to go once they hit the ice. It's hard to service them up there in Yellowknife. You don't start until the middle of January, and by then, you've got six feet of snow on top of them, and you've got to shovel them out. When it's 40 below, and you're trying to get a truck running, it's not good for it. I baby my equipment and make sure everything is looked after. If you go into my shop, you'll see every tool you have ever dreamt of. When it comes to equipment, I spare no expense. I have a 50-ton air jack, along with a full set of air and master mechanic tools. I do my own arc or stick welding, and I even have my own track machine and water tank in there. You'll see my boat in there. Everything is neat, clean, and put away. I pride myself on how I keep my machines. You can run my vehicles for five years on the winter roads, and they will look and drive like new.

My shop is pretty terrific, if I do say so myself. For starters, you can put a good-size airplane in there, which is what the building was actually designed for. The structure is constructed entirely of aluminum, and measures 80 feet long by 50 feet wide. It's 7,500 square feet with a ceiling clearance of 18 feet. I bought the structure as a kit and put it together myself. There were thousands and thousands of rivets and bolts, which took a week to put in. I had to hire all the kids in the neighborhood to help out.

Cold weather makes the ice roads possible and nothing can run until it gets cold enough. One time we didn't get going until February 14 or 17, and we were done by about March 27. There weren't many loads and everyone lost money. It was devastating. So, you need the cold but it's also something you have to deal with every day.

Of course, you don't just show up in January with your rig and hop out onto the ice and have at her. Dozens and even hundreds of hours go into getting ready before you can even get your first taste of 60 below zero. No truck can stand up to the Arctic until it has been custom-prepped for running nonstop for 1,700 hours straight in the coldest temperatures on earth. Getting ready means inspecting every hose for cracks or leaks and testing every single plug. I install belly tarps under the engine to keep warmth in and moisture out. I started getting my rigs ready back in October. By early December, I'm locked and loaded and ready to hunt ice.

If it's really cold, I use about half a cup of automatic transmission fluid or two-stroke engine oil in each tank of fuel. When the temperature isn't so cold, say, 30 below, I do it about every other trip. I also use Arctic air lines. They're just rubber but as expensive as anything, so I just make my own. For the fifth wheel, most guys put grease on them, which is fine for average cold weather but when you get into 40 or 50 below, that grease just makes things worse.

There are lots of little things, little tricks of the trade, that become second nature after a while. For example, I also dip my fuel filter in methyl hydrate once at the beginning of the season before I fill it with diesel fuel. Methyl hydrate is a very poisonous, very flammable alcohol that comes from wood. It smells like the kind of alcohol people can drink and is supposed to taste even sweeter, but drinking just 1 milliliter can make you blind, and less than a shot glass can kill you. The methyl hydrate dries out any moisture you have in the lines, which is one of the main reasons for breakdowns and mechanical failures on the ice roads. Most people will tell you that you're soft in the head for doing that, but fifteen years ago, I learned that trick from a diesel mechanic from one of the mines. Taking time for all the tricks can keep you rolling when it's 50 or 60 below. Over the years, I learned this kind of stuff can make or break you. It's the difference between eating steak and eating hot dogs.

There are other things you can do, like use a diesel fuel

additive, either cetane boost or Ski-Doo oil. Both of those will keep everything lubricated. Nowadays, diesel doesn't have sulfur, so you have to keep your cylinder walls from drying out. As far as my personal gear goes, I use Bamma shoe inserts made out of fiberglass, which is a must for running the ice roads and can keep you from losing your toes. I also wear coats made by Carhartt. They'll stand up to wind, oil, water, and are nearly impossible to rip or tear. You can really work in them. My hat is rabbit and I wear a few different types of gloves, depending on the weather and the work I might be doing that day. They're all top-of-the-line and cost a bit.

After a while, you don't really even notice the cold. It becomes just part of the job. Of course, most people will never in their lives experience the kind of cold we've got here. I've worked when it was 72 below zero. At that temperature, steel can shatter like glass. It freezes and gets so brittle you can break it with a hammer.

Lots of things can happen out on the ice, and most of them are bad.

9

DASH FOR THE CASH

 ou'd think that when it comes to ice, the colder the better, but that's not the case. Ice is as susceptible to extreme temperature as any other solid. It can become brittle after a while, and surfaces that were nice and smooth just the day before will open up huge cracks two or three feet across and maybe a hundred feet long. That's a problem when you hit mid-season and the temperature has been at 40 or 50 below for several weeks straight. Get your front tire in one of those cracks and the jolt will throw you right out of your seat. You've always got to pay attention to the ice. It can mean the difference between life and death.

When it's just a little bit warmer, you get better ice. I like 30 below, because at that temperature, crews can flood the road with water and make road-ready ice that's smooth and free of cracks. Our trucks pound the ice up and down non-stop, which makes the ice thicken. Day after day, the weight of the trucks hauling loads pushes the ice down, deflecting it into the water, where it will add even more water. All that bouncing down and springing back up builds the ice, so you're able to haul bigger and bigger loads until you reach a max of 180,000-pound loads. That's the equivalent of about twelve elephants pounding across the ice.

As soon as the season heats up, the freight yard, what we call "the pit," will run 24/7 with trucks going in and out by the dozens. The pit is a giant, 50-acre rock quarry where a few thousand loads in various shapes and sizes are parked all over. It sure is something. The wind ships and moans through the long corridors of steel, making it like no place else. From the air, it looks like the world's biggest set of kids' blocks has been strewn about amid the snow. From the ground, all you see is a long line of loads. It's just load after load after load. . . . The space is so big that forty or fifty trucks can get in there to tie down at once. Freight has been arriving mainly from Edmonton for the past ten months or longer. I say "longer," because there are always loads that never made it out of the yard last season. Either the year ended early or the loads were low priority. At the start of the season, you look at all of those thousands of trailers and it seems impossible that anyone can move them out in just eight or nine weeks. But our small army of drivers will do just that.

You go to the yard with your order from dispatch and the pit manager will give you a trailer number. He might say: "This load weighs forty thousand pounds," give you a trailer number, and then direct you to that load. Loads are separated by weight. So all the 40,000-pound loads will be in one area. You'll hook onto that 40,000-pound load, tie it down, and that's your job. You're limited by the weight capacity designated for the ice for that particular day. So if the capacity is 40,000 pounds, you can only haul loads of that weight or less. There might be another load that looks about the same but weighs 41,000 pounds. It's only 2.5 percent over the limit, but no dispatcher or pit manager will let you take it. As the season moves on, heavier loads will be cleared by the ice road monitors. That's good news for us, because heavier loads mean more money.

Aside from the weight classifications, the mines prioritize what freight needs to be delivered. Replacement parts for a rock crusher might take precedent over a load of concrete one day. A week later, the opposite might be true. It all depends on what's going on inside the mines. If something urgent is needed and you're on deck, you'll have to strap on and drive off. The dispatch system is very simple: all orders have a number and a priority ranking from low to high. A dispatcher matches an order with a truck number, a trailer number, and a tee or departure time. That's it. If there's no priority item for the mines, then the dispatcher just starts cleaning out the pit. When that happens, a driver will have more say about which load he wants to haul. Sometimes you'll get drivers who won't haul certain materials. "Oh, I don't want to haul pipe," they'll say. Or, "I'll be damned if I'm gonna haul steel all the way to Ekati." They won't want to haul those things because the loads shift and they don't feel comfortable. A load can feel "uncomfortable" if it isn't balanced or hasn't been loaded properly. A load that is back-heavy, for example, will cause a truck to ride high in the front, which will result in loss of traction, since the tires won't be pressing down with their full weight onto the ice. So you'll slide around and struggle with turns and going up hills. Those loads can be rough going, especially on the portages.

Many drivers don't like to haul loads where the weight isn't balanced. Odds-and-ends loads, for example, are irregularly shaped with a lot of space between the cargo. That makes balancing tough, which is why some drivers refuse to haul them. Me, I haul anything and everything and I've never lost a load. I've been put to the test a few times, though, I can tell you. Once, a load of pipe was sent up from Edmonton, which barely made it to Yellowknife in one piece. That was over a highway—not even an ice road. The load arrived dangerously off-balance, dangling over the driver's side by more than 3 feet and over the passenger's side by another foot. The yard supervisor took one look at it and shook his head as if to say, "What the hell am I going to do with this?"

"We've got nothing to reload that pipe with," he said, turning to me. "Can you make it up there?"

I walked around the load a couple of times. "Well, I'll strap her down and give her a shot. But the way she's hanging . . . we'll have to give her the wide-load designation."

"Of course, of course," he said.

Wide loads come with bigger paydays, so I wasn't playing around. I strapped those pipes like my life depended on it, which it did.

I hit the road, hawk-eyeing my mirrors and keeping my

radio close. I kept calling out over the radio, "Wide load coming. Wide load coming!" And of course, everybody I met answered back, "Hugh, your load of pipe is about to fall off." With the truck pulling hard to the left the whole way, it was like my bull-riding days all over again. Somehow I got halfway up the road when I remembered a pit where they were keeping sand and a loader. I pulled in, and sure enough, the loader was just sitting there. I'm an equipment operator, so it was nothing for me to grab this machine, bat my load back straight, and strap her down again. Now I had a nice, regular load, but I still got paid extra for the over-dimensional load designation. Nice work if you can get it.

Besides the weather, storms, and sleep, the thing that can slow you down is loading and unloading. How long it takes to unload depends on what you're hauling. Say you're hauling loads of pipe—well, with pipe they just come in with a big forklift and take it off. Or they sling it and crane it off. Shacks—portable bunk houses for six or eight people—are the same thing. When you have cement, say twenty-four bags at 2,200 pounds each, that's a nice, quick unload too. It's all forklift. Sometimes a van takes longer, because the loading crews have to drag each item out of the back and then haul it to a designated area. The driver doesn't touch the contents of a van, but it's his job to unchain and unstrap an open load.

If you don't feel comfortable with a load, you shouldn't take it, but you can't always have the gravy loads either. You can't just take something like a trailer or van where all you do is back under it, roll up the legs, and away you go. We call those gravy loads, because you don't have to strap down an open load, so you don't lose the considerable time that it takes to load and unload. You pick it up easy, and when you arrive at your destination, you park the truck and go to sleep. The crews will unload the van and bang on your door when they're done. Gravy. But when you haul anything else, you've got to take your time loading it, and then after you've reached your destination, you've got to get out, remove all your straps, and roll them up. By the time you get your straps rolled up, the unloading crews will have just about finished pulling freight from your truck. You've hardly had a chance to catch your breath, never mind catch some shut-eye. Another truck is waiting right behind you, so you have to hit the road. I don't mind strapping a load down, but it's nice on the aching bones to get a van once in a while. I probably get four or five a year. Fine by me. I'll mix it up, as long as I keep moving.

With the season in full swing, every load is crucial cash in your pocket. Time is always short, so you've got to work hard and you've got to be resourceful. One time, I drove 2,400 miles with a rope tied around an alternator, knotted up to keep it in place. It worked fine as long as I didn't torque the engine too much. Another time, I broke another belt, only to realize that I had loaned out my rope. I had to jury-rig the repair with a pair of socks. I've had floor heaters go out, which caused ice to form around my feet. In that situation, I used duct tape and cardboard to redirect the flow of air from the vents of an upper heater to the floor. Nobody said it was going to be easy.

round mid-season, you become especially aware that the opportunities to make your personal earning goals are starting to run out. You sense that sand going through the hourglass. I can make $70,000 or more in two and a half months, and that's just my truck. I also get a percent of every load delivered by my three drivers and the trucks they drive. Few jobs on the planet can allow you to make that kind of money by sheer will and determination. Midway through the season, it hits every driver that if he wants to hit his mark, then he'll need to step it up. That's the "dash for the cash." You might have taken your time in the early weeks, but now the race is on to get payloads, so you deliver them as fast as possible. Of course, there are drivers who treat the ice roads like any other job and don't get caught up in load counts and such. With six hundred of us on the ice, some aren't even aware of the race except in a casual way to discuss how their season is going. That's fine. The ice roads have enough room for marathon racers and fun runners alike.

I always volunteer to take a little extra risk because of the added pay. Bigger, heavier loads are no problem for me. Machinery, especially engines—that's the heaviest load, by far. Of course, I like the easy ones too. Hauling cement and ammonium nitrate (a powerful oxidizing agent used in explosives) is about as good as it gets. Cement and ammonium nitrate take a little more strapping—a couple of dozen straps per load—but once secure, they ride nice and stable. They settle in and don't shift around.

Junk loads can be a mess. The loaders just stack the

freight any way they can get it on the trailer, but it's up to the driver to strap it down and make it stick. That's difficult, especially if you're hauling different kinds of metals along with pieces of equipment for conveyor belts, etc. Of course, the longer you're out in the wind, strapping, the higher the risk of frostbite. Unloading is even more backbreaking. Imagine taking a few hours to move around 1,000-pound crates after you've been driving for eighteen hours straight. Clerks at the mines use forklifts and cranes to do the unloading, but they can't get started until you pull off all of your straps and unchain the load. After driving for maybe ten hours in a storm, everything is covered with ice and snow. It's a hell of a job to get it off. Everything is stiff and heavy and practically welded together. Of course, your job is that much more difficult when you're tired. A couple years ago, TJ Wicox, one of the other drivers featured on the TV show, was tying down a load with a load binder. The load binder snapped open while he was still hanging on to it. TJ crashed into the truck behind him. He started feeling severe abdominal pain while on the run and was forced to struggle through the rest of his delivery before he could receive medical attention. Eventually, TJ had to be medevac-flown to a hospital in Yellowknife. Poor guy.

Oversize loads pay a lot, about 35 percent more than a regular load, and that's saying something. The largest load I've hauled up there is probably a fuel storage tank with a capacity of more than 6 million gallons and more than 35 feet high. Custom ice roads had to be built so I could complete the trip. We had to take down power lines along the way so we could pass through, then we had to lift all the phone and utility wires when we got into town. That's not your average load. Not by a long shot.

Oversize loads can be unwieldy, heavy, or both. With unwieldy loads, you have to watch your crosswinds and clearances. With heavy loads, you worry about weight distribution, going up and down hills, and your speed in relation to the thickness of the ice. Of the mega-loads, anything to do with rock trucks and their parts is the heaviest. Rock trucks are off-highway vehicles used to transport huge amounts of dirt, rocks, and coal across unpaved roads in open-pit mines, or on construction sites and gravel pits. These trucks, even empty, are too heavy for public roads, and typically carry loads of 100 to 300 tons. For transportation, they must be broken down into various parts and put back together at the job sites. That's where I come in.

For twenty-five years, the Titan held the title for world's biggest truck. Nowadays, Caterpillar makes the biggest. Those 797s are capable of hauling upward of 400 tons. They run about 48 feet long and 35 feet wide. That's just the box and nothing else. I've driven these bad boys on the ice roads.

If you want the extra money for the tricky loads, you have to know what the hell you're doing. Another big load I carry is the B-train. B-trains are what we call super-Bs. They're the same thing, and you hear the names used interchangeably. A super-B is two trailers attached with eight axles and a fifth wheel. That fifth-wheel coupling is located at the rear of the first trailer and is mounted on a tail section above the lead trailer axles. Each axle is designed to carry up to 20,000 pounds, so you're hauling 160,000 pounds. That's about three times more than a regular truck. They run at least 113 feet and then some. The super-B is a little more stable than other twin-trailer setups you might see elsewhere. That's its main advantage.

I especially like pulling super-Bs. The two connected trailers will follow you real nice. With a super-B, you're pulling a tandem axle more than 50 feet long. You have to take all your corners wide, so your back end doesn't run over everything and you have to have a little more power. You also have to have the know-how to make the haul. If you screw up, you have to back up two trailers. Now, there's a trick.

Dynamite, gas, fuel, and propane cylinders are all hazardous loads, but you don't get paid any more than any other load. I guess the mines figure that bulky or oversize hauls pose more risk than chemicals or explosives that have been packed and loaded securely. I have no problem carrying whatever the freight yard is willing to give me—I just make sure my load is secure so that I don't have to stop on the road and re-strap it. I've broken crates by strapping them on so tight, but that's okay. Just as long as they're secure. It's all about balancing the load, too. An extra chain here, an extra strap there makes a big difference. You have got to make sure it's done right. Say you have hazardous materials, like bags of dynamite, ammonium nitrate, and you lose it—it falls off your truck and you lose it.

Dash for the Cash

Well, that spill creates a dangerous situation, an environmental hazard, and a big hole in your pocket. Security is going to find it and then find you. You'll have to pay to have that cleaned up—one spill could cost you $20,000. There go your earnings for the season.

Driving through the portages is a wild ride, so you better make sure that you feel safe with your load on there. Some of these guys strap her down the same way as if they were going down a four-lane highway. You can't drive on a portage like that, because the load will shift, which, in turn, will rock the truck. Pretty soon they're upside down somewhere.

The roads are privately owned by the mines, and the security patrols that have been around on the ice roads for the last dozen years or so work for the mines too. They're always out on the ice to make sure that the loads are properly strapped down, that speeds and following distances are observed, and that drivers are going in groups of at least two. You aren't allowed to travel alone (if something goes wrong, a lone driver has little chance of getting help), and you aren't allowed to follow behind another truck closer than half a mile. If you follow too close, your waves could create a pressure blowout that will burst right through the ice. Plus, if a truck goes down and you're following too close, you're going to go down too. Brakes are useless on ice and you won't have time to stop.

I know the guys who maintain the roads and I know all the security guys. They're all retired Mounties, but they're not up there to be cops. They're up there for safety. "No speeding, no passing, no fucking around," they'll say. I've known them all. They're good to me and I'm good to them. They'll tell me if one of my drivers has to be reprimanded. They know that one way or another, I'll deal with a driver who isn't obeying the rules of the road.

By mid-season, four thousand to five thousand loads will have been hauled across the ice, which will make the ice thicker and stronger. Sometimes, however, a road can suffer from overuse. Maybe there's a weak patch that hasn't healed properly. In that case, road builder Nuna Logistics will close the damaged area and reroute through traffic while the crews nurse that section back to health. Many aspects of road-building are high-tech, but when it comes to designating a closed section, workers will just block it with a row of giant snowballs spray-painted fluorescent orange. You've got to see it. It looks so out of place, as if graffiti artists were turned loose to tag up the tundra. I guess if Ben and Jerry came up with a new flavor of ice cream based on the ice roads, that's what it would look like.

Nuna does a lot to make sure that the roads are safe and strong. The only thing they can't control is speeding. If you're driving a heavy load and speeding, you're just asking for trouble, because the heavier you are, the bigger your wave. Those big waves erode the ice, and if they hit a dead end, they can explode right through. Some speeders get away with it for a while. It's all fun and games until something goes wrong. It might be okay on the strong ice that forms on deeper lakes, but not all lakes are deep. Some have reefs, shoals, and currents that keep the water moving, creating thinner ice. Shallow water is more likely to have algae that absorb sunlight, which results in fluctuations of water temperature and creates little pockets of relatively warm water, called "hot spots." We experienced drivers know to drive over these kinds of lakes with extra caution, but rookies don't know or care. The consequences can be deadly.

If you're driving down the ice road and you see a pothole as big as a manhole cover, then you know that somebody was speeding and blew that ice wide open. A section of ice may be 4 or 5 feet thick, but when that wave hits, it's still going to explode like a bomb and pop that ice right out in huge chunks.

Twelve years ago, I was out on the ice and had a guy fly by me. He was driving a fuel tanker truck with tandem tankers, a super-B. Not only is that a massive load but it's not completely stable, because the liquid sloshes back and forth, especially when you're rumbling through the portages. Some portages can be steep, with rough grades as jagged as broken teeth. They can put a truck right on its side.

I'm loaded, too, backhauling and headed south. I'm going the right speed, 20 miles per hour, pushing my energy wave in front of me. I do a mirror check to make sure all my tires are rotating and haven't locked up. When I look up again, I see this super-B heading north. He's approaching too fast, barreling down on me. I reach for the radio but I have no time. Before I can react, he's blowing right by.

Everything happens in the blink of an eye. Immediately, there's a sound like you hear on an artillery range. Bam! His wave and mine have collided. It was like someone detonating a bomb between us. The ice between us explodes. The ice is more than 3 feet thick, but it just ripped like paper. Chunks of ice the size of caskets and water shoot up like a geyser, leaving a gaping hole of ruptured ice all around us.

The rear of his super-B goes down into the hole. The weight of the load is dragging his rig backward. The tail end of the truck collapses into the hole and stops. It's dangling in the water. I'm alive but that can change at any minute. Cracked ice and part of the hole extends out in front of where I need to go. I'm stopped dead, stuck 20 feet away on the other side of the blowout, positioned laterally to him. The ice around us is still heaving, shifting, and cracking with seismic after-shock.

I jump out of my truck. I'm blind with rage.

"Get out of that truck! I'm going to beat your head in!" I shout. "You just about killed us both."

Lucky for him, a security patrol comes racing up in one of their light trucks. They must have been chasing this rig. I've never seen them move so fast. One of the guys grabs the driver and pulls him to safety—both from the hole and far away from me. I'm bellowing and still furious. I keep away from my rig in case the ice gives way. They call in another truck to pump out the fuel load in the super-B. Next, they tow the trailer out of the hole. They decide that it's safer to leave my truck in place and let the ice heal around it. The road repair crews pump water from below the ice and try to build it up thick enough on the side. You can't take a chance driving on the side before they've built it up. It could be anywhere from 36 inches on the road but only 18 inches on the side. That's not enough to drive over with a loaded rig. If it's 40 below, you can build 6 inches of ice in twenty-four hours. At 25 below, you'll only get 2 inches. At extreme temperatures, water starts coagulating as soon as it has contact with the air, but even in the Arctic, it takes some time to make ice. I was stuck for thirty-six hours and couldn't go anywhere. I sat there and watched precious hours slip away.

Nine times out of ten, if a pressure blow bursts in front of you, you're dead. Brakes are useless on ice, so you have no way to stop in time. You're going into the hole. Controlling your speed is your only protection. Some drivers risk it, thinking they can gain some time, but it causes more problems than it's worth. I don't need to speed. I have other ways of keeping an edge.

To really succeed in this game, you need to be smart, and you can't be a hot rod. I try to be smart. My truck needs good fuel and I do too, so I eat well and that provides me with an advantage over the other drivers. I eat two big meals a day. I'll give myself a nice breakfast but skip lunch in favor of quick sandwiches or snacks that can keep me going for the rest of the day if necessary.

When I can manage it, supper is my other big meal. I love a nice cut of meat or fresh fish, soup, salad, vegetables—basically the works. I never pass up steak night, if I can help it. Mainly, I live off of wild-game jerky that I make myself or buy from a meat market in Yellowknife, which my brother-in-law Terry Green half-owns and my niece Shylo runs. Most of the guys eat in the camps after every haul, because the food is hot, plentiful, and free. But big meals take time to eat, especially when you start socializing and enjoying all the warmth. A driver might figure on a thirty-minute food stop, but then he gets gabbing and next thing he knows, two hours have passed. Worse, big meals make you sleepy. So now the driver throws in a nap or figures, "Ah, hell, I'm done for the day. I'll finish the drive back in tomorrow." That's why I avoid the camps. Free food can end up costing you big-time.

If I don't eat when others eat, my other advantage comes in the shut-eye department. I just don't sleep as much as everybody else. Ever since I was a kid, I've only needed about five hours of sleep each night. Doesn't matter how long I've been running or how tired I am, five hours is all I need. A lot of guys will pull a long shift but then they'll sleep for twelve hours. What's the point of that?

I keep a tight schedule, which is another reason I skip the socializing that goes on in the camps. I like to push on past the camps and sleep in the portages. That gives me an advantage of a few hours where I can get back early, load up, get my departure tee time, and then head out. Guys will be ahead of me on the road but hole up in the camps for the night. I'll pass them sometime in the night, and then pass them again in the morning. They'll be heading to Yellowknife with two hours to go and I'll already be on the ice, heading north. I sometimes push on to Yellowknife. I'll arrive at 10:00 or 11:00 in the evening to get my next load from

Dispatch and make sure everything is set for a 5:00 a.m. departure. Because I never sleep more than five or six hours, I can ask for an early tee time and get it, because they know I won't oversleep. I just need the five or six hours to be fully rested.

Around mid-season, four or five weeks in, sleep becomes a big issue for a lot of drivers, one that they will have to deal with for the rest of the season. You're going seven days a week for a month straight, and guys wear out. I knew a guy who got so bone tired, he passed out for twelve hours. Next day it was noon or so, and when he went to put on his boots, they were full of what he thought was water. Turns out he pissed in his boots in his sleep. He had just the one pair of boots at that. People do some crazy shit when they're that tired.

I sleep better on the ice roads than anywhere else. Forget the Plaza Hotel in New York—just give me my little bed in the back of my cab with the snow flying and a 40-mile-an-hour wind rocking me back and forth. Usually, I'm so tired that I hit the ol' workbench like a felled tree and I'm asleep as soon as my head meets the pillow. Rarely do I dream. I'm sleeping way too hard for that. Out on the ice, even sleep is stripped down to its most necessary component of restoring the body. Only when I'm back home in Kelowna do the dreams start up again and make for a restless night.

There was a guy I called "Sleeping Jim." He journeyed 5,000 miles from Newfoundland but couldn't go more than 50 miles on the ice roads before he'd have to take a nap. Sleeping Jim was one of the most amiable people I've ever met. He would be all gung-ho at the start of the season: "I'm going to make her all the way this time, Hugh, I'm going to make her all the way!" Apparently, he had a very different understanding of what "all the way" meant.

Sleeping Jim would leave town with his load. From there, it's about 50 miles out to the ice. Fifty miles would put you in the Meadows, 2 or 3 miles onto ice, and basically the starting line to the ice road—which is right where you'd find Sleeping Jim crashed out and sawing wood in his truck. Eventually, he'd wake up and slowly make his way to the Lockhart camp, about eight hours from the Meadows, and there he'd stay. That would be the conclusion of his workday. You'd be on your way back from a delivery, and Sleeping Jim would be snoring it up in Lockhart.

One year he managed fourteen loads to my thirty-five. He was pretty excited because that was a new world record for him. On the last days of the season, it was worth it to track him down, and if you could keep him awake with a cup of coffee, he would have a hilarious story, explaining how he was able to persevere for that fourteenth load. He could make everybody on the radio roar with laughter. That was Sleeping Jim, the Rip Van Winkle of the North.

People can actually survive on less sleep than what they do. Your body just gets accustomed to it. It's like getting used to the cold. If I'm tired, I might flop down in the back of my cab and have a ten-minute nap. That ten-minute catnap will feel like eight hours of sleep to me. I'll wake up refreshed and away I go. Sometimes I've stopped on portages, and if it's a dangerous portage and I'm too tired to clear it, I'll pull over and rest for a few minutes. I'll close my eyes just long enough to get my edge back and then finish off the portage. I figure that it's best to push through and then get to where you can take a longer break. Most drivers will pull it over as soon as they feel the slightest bit tired, leaving themselves with a big chunk of driving to do when they wake up. When I start to feel tired, most of the time I push right through it. I've learned from experience that the feeling only lasts about fifteen minutes. If you do whatever you have to do to stay awake, you'll be fine.

Working in cold temperatures really dehydrates a body and can wear you down, so I keep big jugs of water on hand. A lot of drivers stay awake by smoking and by drinking lots of coffee. As a former smoker, I know that regimen takes its toll eventually. Still, there are lots of things you can do that will keep you alert. Sometimes I'll jump out onto the running board of the truck. A face full of frigid Arctic air will cure you quick. I keep a set of weights in the truck to keep my arthritis at bay. There are times that I'll grab my weights and pump out a set to get the blood flowing and get my energy back. Anyone can do it, but most don't. At the first sign of a yawn, they pull over and go to sleep.

I've never been afraid that somebody's going to beat me or my records. Competition is fun, but I'm there for the cake, which is the money that you can put into your jeans if you're willing to put your mind to it. If somebody can beat me, my hat is off to them. Anybody who drives with me for any length of time, I have to share most of my tricks of the trade with them, otherwise they can't keep up. Funny thing though, even when I tell them everything, most still can't do it anyway. I know my way around machines but I drive by instinct, which I've learned is something you really can't teach. That instinct grows with experience, but even then, there's something deep inside of you, a feeling for the road that you have or you don't. Sometimes I make mistakes but I've survived every one of them. I never second guess myself.

I've never met anybody who can actually keep up for much more than a week. After seven days of nonstop running, they've got to have a break, and then they might come back in a couple of weeks and try again. One season, a trucker named Ben tried to keep up with me. After a few weeks of some long, hard runs he got so tired that he hit the snowbank and completely pulled his bumper off. Ben's truck had to be winched out. He ended up in the snowbank seven times in eight hours, which I think is a record of some sort. Ben was a tough guy, but out to lunch and in beyond his capacity. Matter of fact, he quit the ice roads after that season.

The worst time of the day for fatigue is right before the sun comes up. The sky is gunmetal gray and has an unrelenting heaviness to it that's tough on the eyes. Everybody gets tired looking at that sky, even if they've only been driving for a few hours. There's about an hour and a half, maybe two hours of gray light, where you start nodding off. Here's the thing, though: if you can get through that early light of dawn, you'll be fine to run for the rest of the day. Guys I run with will try, but just as we're about to make it, they give up. I'll call them on the radio and encourage them to hang on for fifteen more minutes, but they throw in the towel, pull over, and go to sleep. It really comes down to fifteen minutes of willpower. Sleeping Jim aside, I'm convinced that everybody has got that in them. If a guy stays with me and I pull him through, he'll have a whole new day in him. But most can't do it alone. They lack the willpower.

Not many people travel with me for very long. I have lots of friends up there, and they know how hard I run and how I don't sleep much. So a lot of guys will say, "Can I run with you for a week, Hughie?"

"Yeah, you betcha," I say.

The guys will drive with me for a week, then bow out and go to bed. Then I see them another three weeks down the road, they'll run with me again for four or five days. Sometimes I'll push them to keep driving. For example, I'll say, "Don, you just stay awake for a little bit longer and you'll be on the ground, and we can go again and get unloaded. And we'll push you to Ekati—get back this far, and then we'll have a nap, and then we'll take off." A lot of these guys take the bait. When they can make five to six loads extra, that's a lot of money for them. You're talking another $20,000 going into their pockets. By the end of the season, it's getting warm, so you can only travel at certain times anyway. Security won't let you travel alone, and since there are fewer drivers on the roads, you have to partner up with somebody. So I have lots of guys up there that I partner up with at the end.

Some drivers travel all year long in a pair with a friend. They just keep company with each other, and they go and go, but I don't. I don't like waiting and stopping for somebody else. When you run with somebody all the time, you have to wait for them to load and unload before you can go. I go like the devil is after me, so standing around doesn't work for me. A few guys have gotten their noses bent out of shape about it, but they're not writing my checks. I'm happy to help other guys out but I usually run by myself. I make way more loads when I run by myself. If there are four guys going, I just jump in the group, and I tag along or lead them up. Then I carry on and unload. I just head back and I jump in with somebody else. People always want to team up with me but there's no use in me trying to sleep if I'm not tired. You're running hard and then the guy says, "Well, I've got to stop and sleep." So now I'm stuck. I used to coach guys into staying awake—the way I do it—and we'd be going along fine but then all of a sudden, they would fall asleep and hit the snowbank. So I decided that wasn't the way to do it.

After trying and failing to run with several guys consistently, I started jumping in with whoever was going. That has worked out much better. Sometimes I'll be sitting there in the camp, because you can't go back by yourself, and all of a sudden somebody will come on the radio and say, "This is such-and-such southbound." That will mean two trucks coming through. I'm all ready to go, so I'll say "Make that three," and I'll join them. Now I've got a ride home, so away I go. When I get down to Yellowknife, I'll tell dispatch that I want a tee time for 2:00 in the morning. I'll go down there to the yard at midnight, get loaded up, and tell them I can leave in an hour. And they'll say, "Okay, we'll get you set up." Pretty soon, a couple other drivers show up, get loaded, and are ready to go, so the yard manager will say, "Okay, now you've got a crew, Hugh, you can take off," so away I go. However, should those drivers want to stop and eat, I'll just carry on and jump in with somebody else.

I've had to stop and wait sometimes, which can be frustrating, but I've never been tempted to go on by myself. You can't, or you'd get run off by security or the other drivers. There are certain spots where you can go by yourself unofficially for a few miles—for example, from BHP to the Diavik turnoff—but most areas are off-limits to solo driving. You can come back empty just so far to some spots by yourself until you meet up with somebody else headed the same way, or you can go from one camp to another camp by yourself, but then you can't travel on your own. Lots of people try to sneak back alone. They think they're going to get another load. But they get caught and then they get banned. For a first-time infraction, you get banned for three days. The second time earns you a five-day ban. If it happens again, you're gone. In five days, you can deliver two or three loads, so that's a lot of money and not worth the risk.

Even if it was legal to travel alone, I wouldn't. It's too dangerous. I've broken down too many times with blown hoses, lost antifreeze, broken belts, or sliced tires. You name it, it's happened. Your truck is done in those situations. What do you do by yourself? The only thing that's going to keep you alive up there is if your buddy's truck is running. If you're by yourself and your truck quits, what happens? It's 2:00 in the morning, 60 below zero, everybody is sleeping, and nobody's coming through. If you break an alternator belt, which happens a lot, now you've got no radio contact. In about twenty minutes it will be the same temperature inside your truck as outside. You're screwed. A buddy means that you've still got radio contact and a place to stay warm. If the cold isn't a factor, then the truck you're running with can get back to town and get you your belt.

I've always been the first one up and the last one out of there. The first and last batches are considered an honor but also the riskiest. Nearly everybody else is gone, and I'm still hauling the last loads in. Nuna Logistics, Tli Cho, and the mines make the call on when the roads are closed for the season, but the decision on whether I can deliver that final load is mine alone to make.

Besides sleep deprivation, bad weather is the other constant of ice road work. Sometimes it shuts us down. The legendary bars of Yellowknife can be the best place to wait out a storm, or the worst. All depends on your point of view. You'll have all the fun you can handle or all the trouble, most likely both. Even so, the bars of today are tame in comparison to the good old days when there would be miners and real mountain men. In most places outside of the Northwest Territories, if you fought, you were blackballed and never let back in again. But in the Yellowknife bars, you could go into a place, have a fistfight, and still be allowed back as soon as you cooled off. There was no shortage of tough guys in those places. One time a guy punched somebody so hard that the second guy's glass eye popped out and rolled onto the floor. The first guy got freaked out and picked up the eye and went to give it back, but the second guy's old lady grabbed it and said, "Did that thing come out again?!"

Dash for the Cash

She threw it into the street. That's just one story among hundreds. Brawling was considered a nice way to break up the monotony of winter.

The Gold Range opened in 1958, but because of its notoriety, people know it as "The Strange Range" or just "The Range." Everybody who goes to Yellowknife makes a stop at the Strange Range. Bad weather and hard drinking seem to go hand-in-hand.

The Range is a dive, just a rough-and-tumble goddamned dive, but to this day, the Range is probably the only place on earth where the women flock and line up to buy you drinks. Mostly they are Indians and big, stout Eskimos who can put an average-size man on their backs and drag them home. These lumbering ladies just can't wait for the ice roads every year. Maybe it has something to do with being such an isolated community, but as soon as you walk in, the eyeballs are on you, then the free drinks are coming your way. After a few, and especially around closing time, they decide you're ready to go home with them. Basically, you have little choice in the matter. Sometimes a bunch will take a fancy to you and then the Eskimos and the Indian women will fight over you. After they've bought you drinks, sometimes other girls will swoop in and try to hustle in on the action. A fistfight between the women usually follows. Whether you like it or not, you are expected to go home with the victor.

As long as you're a regular, you're pretty safe. But if you're new to town, you should see the women's eyes light up. I've dumped a lot of drivers off at the Range over the years, especially during a big storm, or when you're shut down because it's getting close to the end of the season and you've got to wait for the roads to freeze up. Guys who have done nothing else except drive for a month suddenly find themselves with a chunk of free time. I laugh when some newbie says, "Have you ever been to the Gold Range?" or "Hey, do you know much about that Strange Range? I'd like to go sometime." I answer, "We'll put it on the list. Don't worry about it." Before a rookie can say "How about a beer at the Range?" there they are—new meat ready for the auction block. None of the women are subtle, either. A standard pickup line might be, "I like to have a baby boy from you." So there are no misunderstandings about their intentions. The fun and games go on pretty much every night of the week. If you get drinks bought for you at the Range, you better believe it's going to be a long night.

With all that in mind, a driver might decide he's better off in a blizzard. When the storm does pass, Nuna Logistics will bring in the plows to clear the roads and then grade them like new. Once the ice road is open again, the other truckers and I will be on the move, trying to make up for lost time and money.

There are a few old-timers like me who work like that and can haul in a lot more loads. Not many, though.

10

SUNSET AND SURPRISE

oad by load, portage by portage, slowly, slowly you start racking up the days and making it through the season. There are times I don't even know what day it is. I know the date all right, because it's on the forms I sign when I pick up and drop off my loads. But I don't have a clue as to what day it is, because out there on the roads it just doesn't matter. The ice doesn't care, that's for sure. Sometimes I won't talk to my wife for ten days at a shot, but when we finally connect, she'll tell me what day it is.

"Sunday?" I'll repeat, astonished. "Holy shit, Dianne! I thought today was Thursday." I don't have a clue. I just know that the season is getting on.

Late March is the high point of this dance with the elements that we've been doing all season. The weather is changing, and our time is nearly up. It's still cold, but the air isn't quite as sharp. It smells a little different. Something in the wind that's hard to describe, like the air is fresh and full with the smell of melting snow and the faintest hint of sodden earth just below the white surface. You start getting twenty hours of daylight. Each sunrise and sunset becomes a masterpiece full of violet, salmon pink, and true gold that can make the ice gleam like polished steel. Other times, the sun will set and fill the sky with waves of deep red and orange, the color of lava. The surface of the ice melts in the new sun and fills in at night. By daybreak, it will be as smooth as a baby's bottom and will shimmer like blue crystal. Any cracks that were there the previous day will have vanished by morning. You couldn't do better if you had a Zamboni.

If you're just about the money, you'll miss the splendor of the place and all the little moments that make you glad to be alive to see what is before you. The beauty of it all, those gifts of sunset and surprise are one reason I don't need to psych myself up to get out there. I've been driving the roads for so long I look forward to going up, look forward to each haul and those small gems of nature in an otherwise long, long day. Still, despite the beauty of it all—despite the fascination—boredom will set in, unless I keep my mind active. So much of the job is a grind and an endurance test, that's for sure. The drivers who came up for nothing more than adventure will be disappointed. These "gung-ho guys," as I call them, don't last, because so much of the job is a grind that you have to endure. Once you get used to the ice and get a handle on the basics of winter road driving, there are long stretches where nothing happens. Gung-ho guys don't stick around long enough to make it through weeks of long days and nights. They're all about the challenge out there but can't handle the challenge that comes from inside.

I always tell all the guys who come up there with me, "You're going to get bored when nothing happens, which is exactly when something is going to happen." When the speed limit on the roads is 20 miles per hour, when the ice is empty and you've been over the same 10-mile straightaway over and over, it gets monotonous. There's the temptation to rig up your cruise control and give yourself a break. One time, I tried reading a book to pass the time. I know. I actually thought it would be a good idea to read a book and drive the ice roads at the same time. I can't remember what book I was reading. Another driver had given it to me and said, "You gotta read this book. It's amazing. You'll like it, Hugh. You really will." Reading usually makes me tired, but he guaranteed this one was a real page-turner.

So I was out there on a beautiful day, when the sun was shining and the ice on the lake was a gorgeous, crystal blue. I'm driving along with the cruise control on, set at twenty clicks. (Cruise control, by the way, is a stick wedged between the gas pedal and the underside of the dashboard. Sophisticated, eh?) Well, I could see for miles and there wasn't another truck in sight. Anybody who was coming would radio in way before they met me, so I figured I was okay. In fact, I thought I was doing just fine. The seats in my trucks all swivel, which makes everything that much more comfy. I was moving along fine and soon asking myself, "Why didn't I think of this before?"

I'm out there, reading this book, watching the road, and living the life of Reilly, and thinking I'm the best thing since sliced bread when all of a sudden, BAM! My truck crashes right into a snowbank. I missed a corner and drove right through a snowbank.

That was it, and it was my own damn fault. I never finished the book or read another on the road.

Two and a half months is a long time to be alone and far from home. You've got to find ways to occupy your time. Some guys like to hang out at the camps or take a few days off and tear it up in the bars in Yellowknife. Others just keep trucking. They listen to satellite radio, read books, watch movies, or play guitars. I guess the wind blowing and blowing with all of those millions of stars above them makes for a pretty good audience. One guy even recorded a country-and-western album with songs about his time on the ice roads. He sang about the ice and the cold and the women he missed. It wasn't too bad.

I have a lot of different scenarios to make the miles pass, and most of them deal with numbers. Calculations and planning, playing with numbers just comes naturally to me. As a kid, I had my own little plot of land, where I grew spuds and took them to market and negotiated a price

Sunset and Surprise

of $6 to $8 a sack. To be successful, I had to map out my whole growing season. Alberta's high altitude, long, warm summer days and cool nights, and plenty of water produced good-quality potatoes with fewer pest and disease problems than you have in warmer climates; however, you only had a one- to two-week window in early May to get them started. As soon as I saw the first dandelion bloom, I knew the soil was warm enough to plant.

Potatoes need to be hilled up as they grow, so I would start them in little trenches below soil level, then keep adding soil throughout the growing season. Hilling—making small mounds of dirt a few inches around the stems of the plants—improves drainage, minimizes frost damage, aids in weed control, and makes harvesting easier. But hilling potatoes is hard work. The ground is hard from winter and you have to whack it with a hoe to loosen it up before you can rake it up around the plants. Wielding my hoe like a battle ax, I would hill up one side of each row, then the other, burying weeds as I went along. If I didn't hill, the tubers would be exposed to sunlight, which would make the potato green and toxic. To some, all of this hard work might have been for chump change, but I had big plans.

In addition to growing potatoes, I used to go with a buddy named Kevin Hill out to the Brazeau Dam and the Rocky Mountains to catch wild horses and bring them home. We never could do much with them outside of selling them as packhorses for hunting, but that would do for us. There were ten thousand head between Brazeau River and Calgary, Alberta, and we'd always run into them on horseback hunting moose. It was a tough way to make money, but we'd try any-thing once. We'd run the wild horses down a mountainside right into a little corral we'd built in the bottom. We'd run them in there, rope them, and then get them on a horse trailer and haul them home. If we got one horse, good. If we got two, better. We'd wear out our own horses chasing these wild ones around.

My dad didn't like horses much, because he had to work with them all his life when he was growing up. So, of course, by the time I was twelve, I was a horseman. Funny how that works. I could break pretty much any horse and always had ten to fifteen head of horses that I'd break and sell. The old man didn't like them much because they chased the cows, so we'd got into it over that a few times, I can tell you.

I've been breaking horses since I was eleven. Much like a trucker who has never driven on ice, I can take a horse that's never seen a saddle and have him ready to hunt in three weeks.

Horses know when you respect them. They sense it some-how. I guess that's why the gentler you are, the better they respond. That's the main trick. You don't beat them to death, that's for sure. A wild horse isn't used to having any weight on his back, so you throw a blanket on him. That's the first step. Next comes the saddle. Never fasten the saddle—just throw it over the horse's back. The horse will buck it off, so you just keep throwing it over his back patiently until he accepts it. If he balks, you go back to the previous step where he was com-fortable and you try again. I might talk to him throughout.

"Easy, fella . . . That's it . . . Let's try that one again, okay?"

Sunset and Surprise

If you keep at it, pretty soon the horse knows you mean him no harm and will be standing there in front of you with the saddle on.

When I learned that (and like most things, I learned it the hard way), I had a good understanding of what patience and perseverance are all about. That's the thing about working with animals. They can teach you a lot . . . if you're willing to learn.

So, you've got the horse in front of you with the saddle on. That feels like an accomplishment right there. Next, you might do up a rope, a cinch rope around his belly, put a bridle on him, and a sack. Horses have sensitive ears and they're careful about anything around their heads. You rub a sack all over their heads so they don't spook whenever something touches their head or their ears. It's all about getting the horse to trust you unconditionally. Once they do that, a horse will tolerate strange sensations and odors that are contrary to their nature.

When a horse accepts the saddle, cinch, bridle, and sack, you're ready to move on.

That's when I'll tie the horse to a post and I'll shoot guns. At first, the horse will buck and snort and be afraid. Pretty soon, though, he's just standing there twitching. After a while, he doesn't even react to the gun. Now you can teach him to handle a rider.

I jump on and just lie over the horse's back. If he bucks, I'll jump off. I'll keep it up—jump on, jump off, jump over, jump off. Pretty soon he's not bucking anymore. Now it's time to throw on a saddle and do it up. When the horse accepts the saddle, you can have yourself a little rodeo. A horse might put up a fight initially, some dancing and snorting, but by this time he's pretty much used to everything else, so it doesn't last long. The horse trusts you. He's got the bit in his mouth. He's used to the weight of the saddle and a man on his back. He's used to sudden, loud noises like guns.

I used to take a new horse into the thick trees once he was comfortable with me on his back. I'd take him into the bush and get him running. He had to go forward, but then he had to turn to avoid a tree. Whichever way he turned, I'd pull the reins that way, so very quickly I had taught him the neck rein. Before you know it, you can give the slightest pull and the horse will turn any way you want. Once you break a horse the right way, he's broke for good and you have yourself a fine horse.

If you spend every day with a horse, you can break him in in three weeks, a month tops. That's a fine accomplishment for just a few weeks' work.

I was twelve when I parlayed my knowledge of horses and markets and selling into a job, helping at the local livestock auction. You could buy everything there, from chickens to lambs, pigs to cows. Anything that was small, like ducks, rabbits, and chickens, would be sold by the piece (per animal) and, generally, anything that was larger would be sold per pound. At twelve, I was big for my age, and strong, too, so I had no trouble hauling around animals and moving cages. Easy.

I would head over to the auctions straight from school and on Tuesdays I would work in Lacombe at the fat cattle sale, and then again Wednesday night at Ponoka. I never went to school on Friday. Instead, I would work at the auction market in Lacombe again all day. At night, I would go to work the night shift at Hannah Seeds in Lacombe. I was still only twelve but could fill 100-pound sacks of seeds at the cleaning plant. My cousin Cory was two years older than me and we worked together at tying off the sacks and loading them onto trailers. We'd work all night and then I'd head to school in the morning. I made $3 an hour hauling those sacks of seeds and quickly became stronger than most adult men.

Right away, though, I decided I needed a truck and started to work on that until I managed to trade the horse for a Datsun. Meanwhile, another horse went toward a hunting rifle, a beautiful .308 semiautomatic that I still own. The gun was worth $700 brand-new, and I traded a horse, right straight across. So, in the same year, I got myself a truck and a gun.

I think of that sometimes when I'm on the road. I think of the past and the future, of how the ice roads are nothing more than a continuation of that planning. I still map out my season and think about what I should do with the money I've made.

Toward the end of the season, when the load counts are going up and up, it's easy to lose track of what you've done. Some guys just go with whatever number the truck company gives them. Me? I'm a stickler for keeping a handwritten record of every load. I know the trailer number, where it went, what the load contained. I make my drivers do the same, because if you don't have a record and they miss paying you for a load, you're out of luck. We don't get our final checks until May, weeks after the season is over. I guarantee that every year, every one of my trucks is off by a load. Everything is computerized, but with everyone running around nonstop and the dispatchers handling more than ten thousand loads, it's bound to happen. If you just let things slide—if you don't keep your own records—well, you lose your bonus for the load and that can be a few thousand bucks. Beyond good accounting, I look at the written records as something of an accomplishment. When the season is over, I'll hoist a beer with my guys and tell them, "See those pieces of paper? That's a record of everything you've done. All your blood, sweat, and tears are right there in your own handwriting. Now that you've made it, nobody can take what you accomplished away from you." I know exactly what I've done with my life just by looking at my records.

My work week ranges from 120 to 126 hours, so I've got lots of time to think. If you're smart and use that time wisely, you'll soon become the master of your own destiny. I can basically program my whole year and make a plan for how the money I've earned can work for me and my family. If everything turns out the way I figure, great. If it doesn't, well, I just go back to my system and make a new plan. That's always what I think about as I'm driving.

"That property at Lake Oseola is undervalued and would make a fine camp. Maybe I can get my brother-in-law to go in on it with me. We could set up hunting and fishing lodges if we can figure out who would run the camp.

"I'm going to put an RV campground on the ridge of

property I own. I started it last year and I'll finish it this spring as soon as I come home. I'll fire up the Cat and flatten everything out. There's at least thirty thousand yards of topsoil there and I get $30.00 a yard for it. That's nine hundred thousand dollars' worth of topsoil right there.

"I'll screen it and haul it myself, which will earn me up to five thousand dollars a day. The topsoil alone will pay for everything else. I'll put in the campgrounds, and when it comes time to sell, I'll subdivide two acreages off this, two three-acre parcels, and I'll keep one three-and-a-half-acre parcel separate and sell two three-acre parcels. I dig all the holes and put in the poles for power and everything else myself. I do lots of work for the local power company and the owner is a friend of mine. I like to buy undeveloped land, sit on it, and when the time is right, sell it for a nice profit and then get the contract to develop it.

"If I can just figure out how to build up my fleet to ten trucks, I can partner with [Ed] to take advantage of that job that's coming up in two years.

"When I get out of here, I'm going to buy an excavator so that I can bid to subcontract on that airport project I heard about."

A company might have its hands full with building plans and permits, so it's easier for them to hand off excavation and road-building to another company. If I can put together a crew and buy at auction for $10,000 an excavator that cost somebody else $26,000 new, then I can offer my services as part of the overall bid and at a fraction of the cost of what the builder would charge. Some of these contracts are worth millions of dollars, which is a hell of a nice return for an investment of $10,000. Of course, it only works if you have the information, lay everything out, and plan ahead. Sometimes I'll get the wheels in motion and then make calls to make sure things are moving along by the time I get home. I may still be working on the ice in March, but I'm already planning my work schedule for June. That's how I look at my life and work: one opportunity that leads to the next, bigger one.

Of course, things go wrong when you take your mind off the road. You can have too much dreaming and scheming. One year, we arrived and the roads had just opened. As the first one to get a load to go up, I was taking a bunch of guys up I hadn't seen since the last year. There was a lot of chatter on the radio with everybody catching up on current events. We made the run without a hitch, dropped off our loads, and were coming back empty. Everybody's excited and chattering away on the radio. Some road builders from Nuna came over the radio and said, "Hey, you guys can take this express lane. Welcome back!" You can go a little faster on an express lane when you're empty. These lanes might only be 3 or 4 miles long, but you can go about 40 miles per hour, which is really hauling ass on ice. You're moving double-time to get back for the next load, which, of course, means more money, so, "Right on!" I'm thinking. We're going down the express lane and I'm grabbing the gear, hammer down, and we're doing close to 50 miles an hour.

There's a big, hard curve where the road and the express lane we're on comes back out onto another road. Usually, they have fluorescent signs that you can see in the snowbanks.

These signs show you that a curve is coming, but we're all flying there and talking on the radio. All of a sudden, it hit me what was up ahead and I shouted into the radio, "Holy shit, you guys! There's a bad curve up here!" I'm going way too fast, and I yelled, "Jesus Christ! I'm not going to make it!" I couldn't slow down. It's ice and there's no braking. No way could I make that turn. If I tried to, I'd be sure to jackknife or roll. The truck right behind me would be in the same predicament and we could have a pile-up. I was in big trouble but there wasn't a damn thing I could do.

"I'm going to hit the snowbank!" I call out. My only hope is to grab another gear and put the pedal to the metal. I floor it, trying to blast through the snowbank as hard and as fast as I can go. These snowbanks are as high as the truck and solid, too. If I'm going too slowly, then I'm going to get buried and stuck. I'll be a sitting duck on the thinnest patch of ice we'll have all season. Everything is happening so fast. I have about three seconds from when I realize my situation to when I hit that wall of snow.

I blast the snowbank and brace for the worst. The snow erupts around me and I'm slammed out of my seat and onto my steering wheel. Of course, under the snowbank is thin ice, and beneath it, open water. I hold my breath and keep the hammer down. There's a crack and rumble, but somehow I make it through without breaking the ice. Had I been going any slower, I'd have gone for sure.

A truck bumper is stamped from a single piece of steel and is designed for impact. But both sides of my bumper were mangled all to hell. I was lucky there was no other real damage. But I wasn't out of the woods yet. The next truck was right on my heels doing the same speed. He had no choice but to follow me into the snow. Had I not accelerated, I would have been stopped by the snowbank and that next truck would have creamed me. Instead, we both sailed through to count our lucky stars. That third driver, though, he was in trouble because the ice ruptured behind the second truck, leaving a patch of open water. Fortunately, he had slowed down in time—everybody else behind him, too—so that they were all able to make the 90-degree corner. Talk about a close call.

Well, we may have managed to avoid wrecking on the first day of the season and we kept that little misadventure to ourselves, but that's not the end of the story. You could clearly see two big sets of tracks going right into the water. To anyone passing by, it looks like somebody went down. I got busy with the season and never thought any more about it. The whole year went on until just before the end of the season, when I broke an alternator belt and had run out of spares. A security guy who was a good buddy of mine came by to assist. We were on the radio to see if another truck had a belt for the same engine as mine. We're driving along, and, suddenly, he slows down and says, "See those tracks there? We figure somebody went down but we have never figured out what happened or who it was. Those tracks have been there for almost two months."

"Well," I said. "I've got to break it to you . . . That was me."

"You?!" he said. He couldn't believe it.

I had to own up. "Yeah. First damn trip up here it happened when they opened that express lane up."

The security guy did a double take and said, "Wow! That's been a mystery that nobody could figure out the whole year."

"That was me," I said. "Mystery solved."

It's not all work on the ice roads. We have a lot of fun, too. You have to cut loose sometimes, and pranks are part of life out there. Usually, we play them on the new guys, but sometimes we get the old-timers, too. For instance, Alex Debogorski from the television series is a devout Catholic. I had a Truckin' for Jesus sticker made up that I put on the back of his truck. The camera guys saw it and you can bet they put it on the show. Next thing you know, Alex was receiving hundreds of pieces of fan mail from baptists and born-again Christians, who all said they were praying for him out there on the ice. I don't know how many hand-knit sweaters he received from little old ladies in Florida. Alex is a big guy, so I just hope they got the size right.

We had another driver, named Jack White, who liked to take some of the newbies under his wing. One night, I was driving along when Jack came on the radio and said, "If you boys have any problems out there and need advice, I'm here to help."

He just sounded so sincere that, of course, you know there was no way I could restrain myself. I got on the radio: "Jack, this here's Charlie."

"Okay, Charlie, go right ahead."

"Well, I got a big problem. I've got my brother sleeping with my wife while I'm out on these here ice roads. What do I do?"

There was a long pause and then Jack answered, "Uh, that's not the kind of problem I meant I could solve."

"Well, could you try?"

Dead silence.

As the hours drag along, sitting in your seat for so long can make you stir-crazy. There are times when we would be half out of our minds with boredom. Sometimes I would be on the express lanes, what we also call the hammer lanes, where you can go 40 or 50 miles an hour when you're south-bound and running empty without a load. Most of the big lakes have these hammer lanes. I would be traveling with Reg or another buddy and we'd get bored, and if no one else was around, I'd say, "Bet you fifty bucks I can make that sharp corner up ahead without slowing down."

Reg would say, "You're on."

If you turned your wheel too fast or too hard, the ice would be slicker than snot on a chicken's lip. You have to time the turn just so. Sometimes we'd both try for the corner, and a lot of times, we'd just barely make it around, but the tires would lose traction and the whole truck would skid across the ice and end up slamming into the snowbank like it was bumper cars. Hitting a wall of snow at 40 miles an hour would really jar your brain. All the way through, you'd be yelling, "Whoa, here we go!"

So either our trucks made it around the corner or your trailer wound up in the snowbank. You would roar with laughter at whoever didn't make it, or roar with laughter because you did.

"You owe me fifty bucks!" someone would say.

"Well, don't sit there with your thumb up your ass. Help me get out of this goddamn ditch!"

Of course, I always carry a tow strap. We would have to pull one another out and carry on. Nobody would be any wiser. The waves of adrenaline would shake up things just enough.

That's just a little game we would play on the way back, when we are empty and the road is quiet.

There are other times when you are traveling in a group and you'd see one of the trucks racing. I'd come up behind, with my lights off, then I'd hit them all at once, so that the speeder couldn't see who was behind him. Then I'd come over the channel, "Security! Pull it over." When he did, I'd say, "Get out of the truck and bring your number."

That meant that the driver was going to be taken off the roads for at least three days. They'd get out of the truck, shaking in their boots, at which point I'd hit the gas and fly by. There they would be, standing on the side of the road giving me the finger.

"That's right," I'd say. "We're number one!"

One time, Alex Debogorski and I were having a little competition and running neck-and-neck for hours. Finally, he fell asleep, hit a snowbank, and had to be pulled out. He was game to keep going, but I phoned in to security. "Truck number such-and-such doesn't look so good," I told them. "He's weaving a little." They thanked me for the tip, then pulled him off the road and made him sleep.

Twenty years ago, I was a much younger man and didn't care a lot about safety. I just drove. Any of us that ran the ice in those early days pretty much had that same mind-set. One time, there were five of us young guys driving together and hauling loads through a blizzard. We made it to the camp at Lockhart only to discover that the road was closed going any farther north. We were fit to be tied. Sure it was snowing like hell, but we had money to make and a job to do. I already had hundreds of miles of storm-driving experience under my belt, going from snowbank to snowbank just to stay in between drifts that could be higher than my truck. It was like surfing in a tsunami, but it could be done, and it sure as hell was fun. I'd drive with my head out of the window, yelling as I went, if that's what it took to see. "Is that the best you've got?!"

The guys were all gung-ho and raring to go, so I came up with a brilliant idea:

"Let's drop our loads here at Lockhart, go back to town, get another load, and come on back up, and then we'll have two loads here. We can shoot out to Ekati Mine as soon as the road opens again. We'll come back, scoop our second loads, and deliver those in the same time that everybody else is still on their first loads. Basically, we'll be at least a day ahead of everybody else."

I was pretty proud of my ingenuity, and the plan worked perfectly. The five of us each had two loads sitting at Lockhart. That's when someone in dispatch let it slip what we had done. I knew this meant trouble because pretty soon there would be a hundred drivers clamoring to do the very same thing, which would create quite a logjam at the camp or somewhere else down the line. I quietly gathered the four other guys and said, "Storm or no storm, let's get the hell out of Dodge."

Lockhart to Ekati is normally an eight-hour drive. With the storm, we did it in twelve hours, then hurried back empty to Lockhart. We learned later that dispatch had refused to release any more loads, and several drivers who had attempted our ploy went empty-handed. It was the dead of night when we arrived back at Lockhart, where everyone was sleeping out the storm. Like ninjas, we quietly reloaded and hit the road again. It was like pulling off a heist.

I knew that the brouhaha would last for a few days, so we skipped Lockhart on the return trip back, which meant holing up on a portage to sleep or bobtailing for seven hours back to Yellowknife with just our trucks and no trailers behind us. That's what we chose to do. The snow was swirling but starting to let up. Meanwhile, the ice was pristine—nice and thick—and we were the only ones on it. It was like being inside a snow globe, and we were laughing like kids and feeling our oats. It was on the last lake before hitting the Ingraham Trail back to town that I was suddenly seized with the urge to spin the wheel and do a donut. Pretty soon we were all doing donuts and figure eights, yipping and hollering. It was Swan Lake with big rigs. If anyone had shown up, we would have been tossed from the ice roads for good, but the snow was covering up our tracks almost as soon as we put them down.

I dealt with some mighty surly fellow drivers for about a week, but at least they never found out about our stunt driving. After that, people either forgot or laughed and said they would have done the same thing and wished they had thought of it first. With that feeling we all had that day doing those donuts, it seemed like we'd all drive forever. Sad to say, I'm the only one of the five who still goes out on the ice. That's Father Time for you.

So that was all when I was young and stupid. I don't advocate that kind of stunt-driving or fooling around all the time, but sometimes when it's late at night, and you've already put in hundreds of hours and thousands of miles, it's just nice to cut loose to keep your sanity.

11

DANCES WITH WOLVES

he Arctic has a brutal beauty that can take your breath away and grab hold of your heart. Lots of people come to see it once and end up staying. They curse how tough it is to survive, but can't see themselves living any-place else. I guess they're seduced by the beauty, by the wilderness and the adventure. I know I was.

I'm kind of partial to the nights. That's when the skies glitter with what seem to be millions of stars. It's like nothing you've ever seen before. It gets so dark up there, but the skies just come to life with all those gems sparkling in the night. And then there's the aurora borealis. That's the name of the northern lights, those incredibly beautiful lights that shoot across the sky in every color you can imagine. The lights take their name from Aurora, the Roman goddess of the dawn, and from Boreas, the Greek name for north wind. The Cree Indians called them "the dance of the spirits." Some people call them the polar lights. I call them awesome.

The lights aren't fixed in one place. They shift and move about. They change colors—from green to blue to red. They even make sounds. You'll hear them rustle, crack, and whoosh, depending on their mood. The Inuit say that they can see their loved ones who have passed in the flickering and the shadows that the lights cast. Dogs will howl and bark at the sound the auroras make, and the Inuit believe they're calling their former masters. I don't know about any of that, but I do know that there's nothing like it anywhere.

The beauty of the North can help you forget the boredom of being cooped up in your truck. But let's face it. The job can seem like a grind when the hours and the miles start piling up. I'm used to it after so many years, but some drivers can't handle the solitude of being on the road day and night. That's too bad, because, by law, you can't have any passengers with you. That way, if your truck goes down, they only have to search for the driver. It's a harsh reality, but that's the way it is. A lot of guys get tired and bored with nothing but the radio for company. It's easy to forget that we're working in a place that few people have ever laid eyes on. It's easy to lose focus, too, but you can't. You have to find ways to stay alert. If I've learned one thing about the ice roads, it's that they're unpredictable. You have to expect the unexpected and all that.

Ten years ago, I was coming back from a run to the BHP Mine when my engine started to lose power. It just choked

and died. I knew from experience that I had moisture somewhere inside my fuel line. A little fuel additive usually pre-
vents this, but this time, for whatever reason, I got stuck. It
was about 3:30 in the morning and 58 below zero. When it's
that cold, all bets are off. Machines and humans will freeze
up in minutes, so you don't want to mess around. I was traveling with another driver, so right away I got on the radio
to make him aware of my situation. He was a fuel-hauler
for ECL. I didn't know him very well, but I didn't care. He
was only about three minutes behind me and that's what
counted.

I fired up my big spotlight and jumped out of the truck
to have a look. My fears were confirmed when I saw that ice
crystals inside the fuel line had clogged the filter and strangled
the engine of fuel. It can happen at any time on the ice road,
but it's more likely in −50 weather. I started by trying to clear
the filter. It was brutally cold, and I was looking for a quick
fix, so I poured a little methol hydrate over it. I managed to
get the engine started again and climbed back into the rig
just as the other driver came along. Two hundred yards down
the road, the engine choked and quit again. Back out into the
cold I went. The other rig tailed behind me, but the trucker
stayed inside while I checked out the situation.

I barely started to work on the filter again when there
was a terrible commotion nearby. Not more than 60 feet beyond my truck, a pack of nine wolves were chasing six caribou, including a calf. Right away, I could tell that the caribou
were exhausted. The wolves had been dogging them for miles,
trying to wear out the young one. Their mouths were hanging

open, trying to get air. The wolves circled and probed. Some snarled and snapped their teeth. Others howled and yipped with excitement.

Food is scarce in the dead of winter. It's likely that the wolves hadn't eaten in days. Now the caribou were making their final desperate stand right in front of my eyes. The wolves were on their hunt and they wouldn't be slowed by anything, certainly not a big rig and a spotlight. I knew that much.

A wolf can lope all day at about 6 miles an hour; then, when he finds something, he'll pursue it for miles at top speed to the point of mindless exhaustion. If necessary, he can rev up to 40 miles an hour to catch his prey when the time is right. And he'll always go for the throat. He'll slash at it—try to open it up—clamp his jaws around it until the animal is dead. I'm a wolf hunter myself. They're one of the easier catches, because you don't hunt them so much as they hunt you. They're naturally curious animals. Fearless, too. You just hunker down and wait. Sooner or later they'll find you.

Wolves will locate a herd of caribou, then probe for the injured, old, or young. As long as the herd stays bunched together, there isn't much the wolves can do, but if they can get them to stampede, the hunt is on. Most likely, these six caribou were part of a big herd, but had panicked and separated from the rest.

Caribou herds in the Arctic can number in the hundreds and thousands. Sometimes they'll run across the ice, and you'll just have to stop your truck and let what seems like swarms of them pass by. I've seen hundreds just lying in the road. I guess they're prone to road accidents. If you hit a caribou with your truck, you have to stop and report it to a conservation officer, who has a little hut on the side of the road. The officer will make sure that the caribou is cleaned and skinned and lined up on the side of the road where they may be randomly inspected for various diseases. At times you'll see hundreds of caribou skins by the road, their flesh being picked at by huge ravens. They can pick a carcass clean inside of twenty-four hours. Nature is brutal but efficient.

I tried to work quickly and quietly on my filter but soon realized that I had attracted the attention of part of the pack. Several looked over my way with their ears pricked up. Jumping back in the cab made the most sense, but it wouldn't solve my problem. With the engine off, I couldn't stay in the cab more than a few minutes. Worse, the longer the engine sat, the less chance of it starting again. It takes a 14,000 BTU heater to thaw a frozen engine block, and that I didn't have. As I tried to make up my mind, three wolves broke from the rest and bounded toward me. I dropped my light and raced for the door. Luckily, the snow was deep off the road and that slowed the trio just enough. I barely made it back inside before one lunged up onto the running board.

"What the hell's going on over there?!" the other trucker called over on the radio. I explained my predicament.

"Just leave that fucking truck and let's get out of here!" he said.

His plan was to blow his horn and hit all the lights. He'd drive up as close to my rig as possible so that I could jump out and into his cab. We'd drive off and leave the truck.

I flat-out refused. "No way," I said. "That'll cost me three days of work by the time I get back here and get the truck running again. No way am I going to do that, not when I can just put in a new fuel filter."

"Okay," he said. "So you don't want to go for help. But if the wolves can't be scared off . . . and I don't see any sign of that happening . . . why don't you jump into my rig and we'll try to wait out the wolves."

That idea had its flaws as well. My engine was freezing up with each passing minute. A new filter wouldn't do the trick an hour from now. My truck could be out of commission for days if I didn't act now and fast. Meanwhile, it appeared that the wolves had brought down the calf and driven off the rest. The three wolves returned to the pack. They would be there for a while. I saw my chance.

"How about you get out and watch my back? You can put my spotlight on anything that moves while I change out that filter."

No dice.

He was too scared. For all the money in the world, he wasn't getting out of his truck. "Well, I'm gonna get this truck running one way or another," I said.

I take great pride in my ability to live off the land. I believe that everyone should own a gun and know how to use it. The world would be a safer place if they did. Our family has always eaten wild game, and supper was always something that we shot. Hamburgers? Forget it. I've hunted everything from black bear to grizzlies to deer to wolves. I thought of that now as I sat there in the frozen night. I owned dozens of

Dances with Wolves

195

guns. It sure would have been nice to have one now. But firearms of any sort are prohibited on the ice roads, so I was out of luck.

Still, even without my guns, I'm always prepared for most situations. This was no different. My pockets were stuffed with roast beef sandwiches, cheese smokies (a kind of sausage filled with cheese), and the homemade jerky I always snack on. It was meant to last me a couple of days, but what the hell. I took a deep breath and, armed with my arsenal of sausages and sandwiches, went back outside. I could hear the driver calling out on the radio, "What in the hell is the matter with you, you crazy son of a bitch?!"

Quickly, I made it to the spotlight I had dropped. First thing I saw were the glinting eyes and the blood-soaked maws of the wolves. Their ears were pinned back as they devoured their prey. It was gruesome. And when I did a head count to see what was going on, when I saw that there wasn't enough caribou for all of them to eat at once, well, I guess you could say I was worried.

A wolf can hear its prey from as far as 6 miles away in the forest and 10 miles over open ground. They can smell a potential meal from almost 2 miles away. They are far more intelligent than dogs, not easily spooked or tricked. But I decided to try. I unwrapped the first sandwich and threw it as far as I could. Just as I expected, a wolf went to investigate. I threw another sandwich in a slightly different direction, then started working on the filter like the devil himself was on my tail. The bitter cold made it hard to maneuver my fingers. Meanwhile, the wolves caught on quick to their unexpected bounty, and by the time I finished with the truck, they were nearly up to my passenger-side door. I was down to two pieces of jerky. I wasn't stupid enough to think that the wolves and I had come to any sort of understanding. Their bared teeth and growls were a good indication of their intentions. The same wolf that had jumped up on my running board now gave me a look like he had figured out a way to get both me and whatever else was in my pockets. My time was up.

"Hey! Back off!!!" I yelled as I backed my way into my rig. "So long, you sons of bitches! Don't let me catch you in hunting season."

Wolves can be bad news for truckers. Ravens, on the other hand, are considered the sacred bird of the North and a good omen for travelers. I'm not sure why they're considered sacred, but I do know that most of the ones I've seen are the size of house cats. If you feed a raven, somehow it will remember your truck. It will fly up and alongside you, drafting for a few miles in the warmer currents that surround your truck. Sometimes a raven will land on your hood, looking for a handout, even while you're moving. They're persistent, that's for sure. I've had one ride on top of my mirror. I'm not much for omens, but sometimes I'll toss a piece of sandwich to a raven just in case.

I've never been superstitious or religious. The only time I go to church is for weddings and funerals, so there are no Hail Marys or emergency text messages to God when I'm in a

Dances with Wolves

rough situation. Most drivers aren't any more superstitious or religious than anyone else, although some of them will cross themselves when moving past a wreck or a ruptured patch of ice. From time to time, you'll have a driver who'll turn a cigarette upside down in his pack for luck, or to change a patch of bad luck. I don't know where the practice came from, but if they really want to change their luck, they should probably just give up smoking.

Shooting stars are considered a good sign too. Other than indicating crystal-clear skies and good weather, I don't know that there's any rhyme or reason other than that they're fun to look at.

The lands of the North are steeped in myth and lore, but most truckers just go about their business. It's hard to remember sometimes that our roads are temporary and will melt to nothing in the spring. Some of the land and water we drive on is sacred to the Inuit and Indians. For that and environmental reasons, a priority is placed on restoration and creating the least amount of impact. As for the spiritual aspect of the land, we truckers aren't known for sentimentality; however, we do honor the ice roads in our own fashion. A while back, I saw a truck stopped on the ice in the middle of a lake. I thought maybe something was wrong, so I tried to get the driver on the radio. There was no answer. As I pulled up, I saw that he was outside of his truck, standing a little ways off. He had some kind of box in his hand and was staring out across the ice. I couldn't tell if something had fallen off the truck or what, so I figured I better check it out. I slowed down.

"Hey there, pal. Everything okay?" I called out.

"Sure," he answered. "These here are the remains of my dad. This is what he wanted."

I tipped my hat to him. "Oh, right on. Well, you sure picked the right spot."

He thanked me for stopping. As I carried on down the road, I glanced back and saw him still looking out over the ice, which seemed to go on and on. The ashes of lots of family, friends, and beloved pets are cast over the winter roads. They dance with the wind and snow until spring, when the lakes finally claim them for all time.

Dances with Wolves

12

PLACE OF MAN

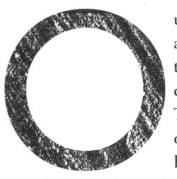utside of the ice roads, most truckers are not accorded much respect. Many think of us as part of the machines we drive, not as flesh-and-blood people. True, we're a crusty bunch and some of us don't exactly think with our heads. So maybe we bring it upon ourselves. But the work we do is important. If we stopped our deliveries even for one day, everything would shut down. There'd be no food in the stores or fuel to run anything. Nowhere is that more true than in the Arctic. Our hours are long and, outside of ice roads, the pay isn't great. I'm not a full-time trucker, but I know that driving so many miles day after day can get to be a grind.

Back in 2008, I'd already logged more than two decades and easily half a million miles of driving on the winter roads out of Yellowknife. I figured I'd pretty much seen everything, but then I landed a job hauling in Inuvik and Tuktuyaaqtuuq on the ice north of the Arctic Circle and 1,000 miles beyond Yellowknife.

Inuvik means "Place of Man" in the Inuvialuktun dialect. That's the right name for the place all right, because the whole town was built from scratch by the government back in 1953. Designed to replace an aging, flood-prone trading post called Aklavik, which was originally built by the Hudson's Bay Company, this little community of three thousand intrepid souls is perched near the Mackenzie River and the Beaufort Sea, as far north as possible on the Mackenzie Delta. The nearest city is Anchorage, Alaska, 650 miles away. Half of the residents, the Uummarmiut, are Inuit Eskimos, descendants of whalers and fur trappers. These Uummarmiut are a tough old bunch. At one time, they would go out onto the ocean in a canoe, be gone for days, and come back towing a whale. At times, the Uummarmiut had fierce battles with Indian tribes, like the Cree, that also lived in the region. "First Nations" is what they go by now, but most people still call them Indians. The Eskimos and the Indians hated each other and waged fierce wars that lasted for centuries. Nowadays, since the creation of Inuvik, they're doing a little better at settling their differences.

Despite its remote location, Inuvik was designed with some important amenities in mind: an airfield, ample fresh water, a wharf, and dorm barracks for the legions of natural gas and oil exploration workers assigned there. Of course, there are also bars for whiling away the long winter nights. When December arrives, the light leaves. Inuvik won't see the sun for thirty days and nights. But the summer months more than make up for the blackout. Come June, the sun doesn't set for fifty-six days.

Building a town from the ground up isn't easy—not when that ground is permafrost. On the hottest day of summer, you can dig just six inches and hit ice. That means utilities like water, waste, and power must be delivered aboveground. Meanwhile, builders have to find ways to anchor buildings from above ground, since traditional foundations are impossible to construct. The engineers have figured it out somehow, because Inuvik has a hospital, a police station, schools, and a sewage treatment plant, just like any other community. There's even a prison and a church shaped like a giant igloo. That's saying a lot for a place that was nothing more than barren wasteland sixty years ago.

Inuvik is as beautiful and as inhospitable a place as there is on the planet. It's the essence of bare-survival living, and not meant for people. In winter, the temperature can drop below −70. The very act of breathing hurts, no matter how well insulated you are. If there's any moisture in your eyes or nose, it will freeze instantly. You'll go to blink and your eyes will freeze shut. Inhale through your nostrils and they'll fuse together. The fiercest winds I've ever experienced were in Inuvik, where the wind chill can induce frostbite within seconds. "Air-cooled" takes on a whole new meaning here.

There's little chance that time and energy would be

invested in Inuvik if there wasn't money to be made. Rest assured, big business has discovered this part of the world, and the business of Inuvik is oil exploration. The oil companies have lease sites right on the Arctic Ocean, where the oil rigs and the camps are set up. The area is thriving, as is Aklavik, the perennially flooded trading post that Inuvik replaced and most folks assumed would float away down the Mackenzie decades ago.

Once in the late '70s, when I was a kid, I did a job for Esso Resources in Inuvik, where I drove a Cat train over the ocean. Cat trains are slow-moving, even in the best of times, but we really crawled along over ocean waves that seemed to have been suddenly flash-frozen in place. It was like they were cresting and moving, then just stopped. At the time, I had never seen anything like it. The job was one time only, and I never thought I'd make it up there to haul a load ever again.

Then came the 2007 season. That year marked the first time I was back driving on the frozen ocean in nearly thirty years. On my drive into town, I passed a ship—not a boat but an actual ship—frozen into the side of the road. That's the first giveaway that you aren't on a lake. Everything is white and exceedingly bright as far as the eye can see. There are no trees or snowbanks or buildings to give you depth of perception, so after a while you get a little snow-blind. Then a tiny speck appears in the distance. You watch it for what seems like forever. Slowly, it grows larger. You can watch that speck for ten minutes before it finally turns into a passing vehicle.

I worked for Northwind Industries and I was driving right out on the frozen ocean. You're not driving on a lake with islands of land in between; you're actually out on the ocean, at the mouth of the ocean, where the waves have frozen even as they crested. Much like pressure blowouts on the Yellowknife ice roads, the ocean has actually pushed up through the frozen waves 30 feet high in places. A wave has broken out and left behind massive chunks of ice. With no land in sight, it's like you're driving on the moon. Even the road signs are different; yes, there are actually road signs stuck right out there on the ocean ice, telling you where to go and what conditions to expect. A sign with squiggles on it, for example, lets you know that here the frozen waves are the most severe. Another sign might post a speed limit of 70 kilometers per hour.

Salt water freezes at a lower temperature compared to fresh water, about 29 degrees Fahrenheit (depending on salinity) versus 32 degrees for fresh water; yet ice over the ocean can be as thick as 7 or 8 feet. That should give you an idea of what the climate of Inuvik is like. Driving over ocean ice sounds a little different from lake ice. Instead of shattering glass, you get more of a booming, like thunder.

The ocean roads are rough enough to throw you out of your seat at 5 miles an hour. The ice is so jagged and sharp that it can actually slit your truck tires wide open. That ocean ice shreds them like nothing. Truck tires pop all the time. That's a given. They get impaled, especially when the ice turns to slush and then freezes again. It can be like driving over butcher knives. Our rigs have eight tires, so we can usually make it through; but if one of your two front tires goes, that's a different story altogether. You could be in big trouble. A tire that blows in the front can slam you right into a snowbank. That's a dangerous situation in a place as remote as Inuvik.

Unlike in Yellowknife, if you're driving in Inuvik, you're likely driving alone. You can also go a lot faster, as fast as 45 miles an hour loaded, which greatly increases the number of things that can go wrong. It's a little colder, the ice on the ocean is a little rougher, and there are fewer trucks. Without a partner, you are truly on your own. It's not enough to be a good driver. You also have to be a decent mechanic and good problem-solver. With all of the bumps, your truck can start to handle as spongy as a water bed.

So, for the first time in twenty years, I was working directly for somebody else and I wasn't my own boss. People in Inuvik only knew me from the television show, which meant I had to prove myself with loads that nobody else wanted to touch. I was the rookie, so right away, I got the shit jobs. Literally. I was driving a super vac-truck with raw sewage from a natural gas exploration site at Langley. Fine by me. I always say that I'll take any job as long as the money is good. Hauling human waste might not be the cleanest load in the world, but it was steady. Each load was 5,000 gallons and weighed 21 tons. My vac truck is insulated. Otherwise, the sewage would quickly freeze into a solid block that you couldn't pump out. When the truck is bouncing over a bumpy grade, it's crashing back down on the ice with great force. If you go to downshift, 21 tons of fluid will slosh violently back and forth, which can build up enough momentum to push your truck out of control.

I started the job by pumping the sewage from a giant heated storage tank into the super vac. It was to be delivered to a holding reservoir in Aput, where the sewage would be treated and recycled. None of that is rocket science; however, inevitably, all of the connector valves, nozzles, and hoses were frozen solid with waste, so I had to have at them with a sledgehammer. When that didn't clear the ice buildup, I used a large propane torch. The cold is so bitter that I could easily wear myself out, so I had to pace myself and give things the time to thaw out. That was essential. No pun intended, I sure took a lot of shit from the guys about the contents of my loads, but I said, "Hey, I'm the busiest guy in Inuvik." That's all I care about. People stopped laughing when I made High Loader for the season.

One hundred miles from Inuvik and just about eight hundred miles above Yellowknife is Tuktuyaaqtuuq, or Tuktoyaktuk, "Tuk" for short, which means "looks like a caribou" in Inuvialuktun Inuit. During low tides, the nearby ocean pulls back to reveal reefs shaped like caribou. One of the Inuit legends tells of a beautiful woman who saw some caribou wading toward her in the water and petrified them with her gaze.

Like Inuvik, Tuk is north of the Arctic Circle, and is located right on the Arctic Ocean. When you think "edge of the earth," that's Tuk. With a longitude and latitude of 69° 27' 0" N and 133° 4' 0" W, it's the northernmost point you can drive to in Canada, yet there are several hundred hardy people who manage to live and work there. Most are Inuit, descendants of whalers and hunters, who subsist today by fishing and hunting caribou. A trip to Tuk is like stepping out from a time machine. You can go months without seeing fresh fruit and vegetables. Char, caribou, and musk ox are still staple foods. Modern conveniences like cell phones don't work, so you have to rely on satellite hookups. A single handset can cost $1,000. Meanwhile, air time can be as expensive as $15 per minute. That's why satellite phone networks insist their users buy prepaid plans, in vouchers ranging from $10 to $5,000.

Can you hear me now?

The Hudson's Bay Company founded a post up in Tuk back in 1936. Companies started looking around the Beaufort Sea for gas and oil in the 1970s, and they're still up there, exploring. Engineers there use special trucks called "thumpers" that weigh 100,000 pounds all by themselves. These thumpers go around out on the tundra and vibrate in order to create seismic waves that locate and measure oil and natural-gas deposits. There might be a group of three thumper trucks that go out, and they would drive a little bit and then stop. They go 100 yards at a time but are spread out from each other by 100 yards. So they're actually covering 300 yards at a time, with each moving 100 yards. Every 300 yards they stop, and they sit there and vibrate. They do a test when they vibrate to see what's under there and if it's worth drilling for. The "thumping" is so intense that it can rattle your ears right off the side of your head. Still, these trucks are far less environmentally devastating than dynamite, which, for a long time, was the preferred method for generating seismic signal data.

In Tuk, tug boats and enormous barges, like the *John Wormlinger*, are frozen solid right into the ice. They can't move them until the spring thaw. In the winter, you drive right up to them right there out on the ocean and do your loading and unloading of bulldozers, machine parts, fuel, gray water from the camps, and whatever else. Some barges are so big that there are barges inside the barges. Everything is frozen into the ice, so you just drive into the barge to load and unload.

The only time you can travel by road from Inuvik to Tuktuyaaqtuuq is during the winter months, from January to about April, on the temporary ice road on the Mackenzie River. The ice road allows for road travel to both Aklavik and Tuktuyaaqtuuq from Inuvik. During the rest of the year, road travel is impossible. Even under the best of circumstances, a haul on the ice road takes five hours to go from one place to the other. Still, you can work in a lot more loads than you can in Yellowknife, especially since you don't have to partner up with anyone. In 2008, I delivered a record sixty-eight loads during the season, versus the thirty-five I can haul in Yellowknife.

The journey is desolate and treacherous. It's breathtaking, too. There's a section called Hurricane Alley, where the winds are so fierce they can crack the ice and cause sea-water to rupture through. Razor-edged potholes abound, as do polar bears. Sometimes the roads are closed when they've been sighted. It may sound like an overreaction, but a polar bear is far more likely to consider humans as food, compared to other bears. They can tear a cabin down to the foundation and rip the doors right off your truck. Your cab is of little protection if you break down and a hungry polar bear is on the prowl.

Weather is unpredictable, especially through the Barrens located on the land side outside of Inuvik and Tuk. Past the tree line, it's just wide-open Arctic tundra with nothing there for hundreds of miles. The wind blows, howls, and shrieks relentlessly. Your truck whips this way and that. The wind never stops, because there's nothing to slow it down. Whiteout blizzards are a common occurrence. There are far fewer trucks running loads up there as compared to Yellowknife, so if your truck breaks down, you've got trouble. You certainly can't count on somebody happening along, and so emergency truck parts, extra food, and water are a matter of life and death. For me, having equipment you can rely on is something I don't mess around with. Thirty-two years ago, I gave an Eskimo lady $50 to make me a pair of seal mukluks. I was just a kid and that was a lot of money back then. She wanted $30, but I knew that she had to chew the seal skin in order to soften and shape them. I gave her the money and then came back for them two weeks later. The mukluks are as good as the day I bought them, and I can still use them today. Worth at least

$1,200 now, the mukluks keep your feet warm, plus you can stand in water and not get wet.

Most ice roads are used exclusively by heavy haulers; however, on the road from Inuvik to Tuk, passenger cars often share the route. The arrangement poses dangers for both trucks and cars. The small vehicles are hard to see, especially during frequent storms or when the snow is drifting or swirling. You could run such a vehicle right off the road and not even know it. Snow accumulates so quickly and so deep that the car might not be discovered until the spring thaw. For this reason, many cars are equipped with bright roof-mounted taillights.

The seismic waves that our trucks generate and push in the water beneath the ice pose another danger. Our waves create undulations in the ice road's surface, which are usually countered by a converging truck's weight or low speed. However, passenger cars are disproportionately light. They also tend to travel much faster and closer to other vehicles on the ice. If the drivers of such vehicles aren't careful, they can get caught by a truck's wave and have the steering wheel jerked from their hands, or their tires bouncing up and down on the ice. For this reason, you'll often see signs posted into the ice that warn drivers to stay a safe distance from trucks.

The area around Tuk has the highest concentrations of pingos in the world. "Pingo" is Inuit for "hill," but these hills are like no other in the world. They are made of solid ice that can rise 160 feet and measure 1,000 feet across, and there are more than 1,600 of these cone-shaped pingos rising against the landscape. Each is at least a thousand years old. Some contain craters in the center and look very much like volcanoes. Mysterious and otherworldly, pingos are formed by underground water that forces up the ground from under the permafrost.

For centuries, the Inuit used the pingos for navigating their way around. They also once climbed them to see the whales, geese, and caribou they hunted. Pingos were good for scouting their enemies, too. As a trucker, you have to drive around them, but seeing these small mountains of ice against the northern lights surely is a sight you won't ever forget.

Arctic sundogs are another phenomenon peculiar to the region. When conditions are right, sundogs will suddenly appear, seeming to encase the distant sun in a huge pale circle of rainbow light. The effect will look like an enormous eye in the sky, with the sun appearing to be the pupil. This "eye" seems to watch as you move like a snail across the jagged ice. Sometimes the sundogs will appear in pairs on either side of the sun, but mostly they encircle it. Sundogs are caused by light shining through ice crystals in the atmosphere. As I approached Tuk in the morning, two bright sundogs appeared— one on either side of the sun. If conditions are just right, these sundogs form a rainbow that circles the sun. Sometimes I've seen them at daybreak, when I was the only driver on the road. It's hard not to feel like some kind of space traveler visiting another planet.

While I was in Inuvik, a natural-gas reserve was discovered at Langley, capable of delivering 1.9 billion cubic gallons per day. They had been searching and testing for several years. I was on the ice, delivering a load, when they made the announcement, and I felt a wave of excitement and pride to have played my small part. Shortly after that, I became the High Loader for the season, and my reward would be the final solo run on the ice before they closed it for the season. I felt like a million bucks.

The ice road season is a long, hard ride. Our bodies ache and our minds drift to faces and places we haven't seen in a very long time. Home, for most, is thousands of miles away, so by late March, when winter gives way to spring, we start to get punchy. We're dead on our feet and anxious to be done.

This change of season marks a lethal game of chance. The drivers are running behind on sleep and they're rushing to get in their final loads before the ice gives out beneath us. That's the time when accidents happen. And they happen to us all. I've flown off the road onto thin ice come end of season. I've done that a lot, at least a dozen times. Luckily, I've never rolled my truck. I've come close, though. Once, I got caught in a whiteout with a super-B full of rebar. It was snowing so hard that moving trucks were covered in more than a foot of ice and snow. They looked like wedding cakes on wheels. It got so bad that when I came up off a lake, I couldn't see past my windshield. I just had to guess where the road was. Snow was swirling all around and drifts covered everything. I was milking my truck the whole way—just trying to keep going—when all of a sudden, I hit a deep drift that buried me in 30 feet of snow. Visibility was so bad I never saw this towering wall of white. I couldn't even open the doors on the truck. Of course, I had to get pulled out.

I fell asleep behind the wheel once too. Now, that was scary. This happened late-season and just after 4:30 in the morning, which is always a dangerous time. The light is changing and dawn is about to break. Somehow, looking at the predawn sky just reminds you of the hour and makes your head nod and your eyes get heavy. I was leading a convoy across Gordon Lake and had been up for thirty-six hours straight. Some tricky weather had kept us on our toes and we had been held up waiting to go. Finally, I was able to make the run but felt tired at the start. Basically, one second I was coming off the ice, driving toward a portage, and the next my eyelids slammed shut and my chin slid down to my chest. I've started to nod off several times but always managed to catch myself in time. This time, I was basically closed for business. I must have been asleep for all of seven seconds, because that's how long it took for me to completely miss the portage and crash into a ditch. I was no worse for wear, but very fortunate not to ram a tree or another truck. At the very least, the ditch woke me up.

By the time we're on those last runs, a certain amount of camaraderie has built up between the drivers. That helps keep things civil. Most of the time, anyway. There will be occasions when two trucks will meet in a narrow portage and one needs to back off and give way. Usually, the drivers will work it out without incident or accident, but a few times you'll run into somebody who's on edge and not thinking straight. You'll be heading northbound fully loaded, which means that you have the right of way and can reasonably expect the other driver to pull over and stop. But maybe this guy is a little punchy and figures, "Screw you! I'm on a schedule!" Or maybe he misjudges the distance and thinks he can hit the accelerator and squeeze through to a spot where the road isn't as narrow. You don't know any of this until it happens, so you're pushing forward when all of a sudden you have a southbound truck speeding through a portage, barreling right for you. I've had some close calls but always made it through unscathed; however, in the final gasp of the 2007 season, my luck finally ran out.

I was driving the Crow's Nest. It was mid-March and unseasonably warm, and the roads were nearly closed. It had already been one of the warmer years, bad news for us. I was going north with a super-B loaded chock-full with 160,000 pounds of ammonium nitrate. That day I was the last one allowed up with a load. I left at 8:00 in the morning, and because I knew that I had a whole convoy coming toward me, I was calling out my portages on the radio. Of course, all the guys coming south had finished their runs and were empty. They assumed that the roads were closed, so they could just burn it home.

"Northbound on eleven," I called out as I started up Portage 11.

I could hear the southbound drivers chattering on the radio. They were all shouting and laughing. They were all talking over one another. It was the end of the season and everybody wanted to know where they were going that night and how they would celebrate. That's all well and good, but they were on a main channel, which should only be used for official business.

No one acknowledged my call, so I was getting a little nervous. I got on the radio again and said, "Hey, you guys. There are loaded trucks coming through here!" I repeated my position. Still, no response. Security heard me, though, and he was trying to cut through all the jibber-jabber and tell the drivers to shut up. His luck was no better than mine. There were a dozen people yelling and laughing and no one could get a word in edgewise.

I came up the hill and around the corner, and there's this southbound rig coming hard off the lake. I had just come around the corner and see this guy cutting the corner so that he won't have to slow down. He's shaving it real tight, but all of a sudden I'm there. I recognized the truck and the driver, so I shouted into the radio, "For God's sake, Hamilton, get over!!!"

He was coming right at me.

Not at my truck, but right at me in the cab.

We were so close that I could see his eyes. Boy, were they wide. He must have been doing 50 miles an hour. I didn't know about time stopping or anything like that, but I said to myself, "I've got to get out of the way!" It was like that time when I was riding on the hood of the Mustang when I was a kid and came close to seeing my life flash before my eyes. I jerked my steering wheel and hit my trailer brakes. It was more of an instinct than a conscious calculation, which is probably a good thing. Everything happens so fast on ice, so either you trust your reflexes and your instincts or you find a new line of work quick.

Say you have a loaded, 100,000-pound truck, and all of a sudden you start sliding. There's no way on earth to stop it, so you're going to have to grab that steering wheel and drive your way out of trouble. That's what happens: Guys will spin out on the hill and the first thing they'll do is grab the steering wheel to try to steer their rig backward. That's a recipe for disaster right there, because chances are they won't be able to keep the rig and trailer straight. They should hit their truck brake first—that's the maxi brake—not their trailer brake. The truck brake will stop just long enough for the trailer to pull them back straight in the line so the truck can come down straight and the driver can back his load down. But most drivers immediately will grab that wheel and try to drive out of it. Nobody can do that. It's a mistake that can be fatal.

Well, on that road, with Hamilton barreling toward me, I reacted with my gut and somehow—somehow!—managed to swing my truck up onto the snowbank. The front end of my truck slammed through the snow full-force. I was sure I was going to die. I was sure we were both going to die. I was coming up there with a full load of 160,000 pounds, so there was no stopping me. No way, no how. That load was in control. That load was pushing me.

If I hadn't jerked my truck at the last possible second . . .

Hamilton was heading right for my driver's-side door, so there are only a couple of pieces of sheet metal between me and his 20,000-pound truck going 50. I would have been dead for sure. But jerking my truck at the last possible second gave us both what we needed, and Hamilton caught the back end of my cab. He tore both my handrails off and cleaved both axles right out from my truck.

But he missed me clean.

I was hurled forward and slammed hard, because of the no-seat-belt rule, but I managed to hold on to my steering wheel. Even so, I thought I was dead.

I reoriented myself and looked out amid the smoking wreckage. Through the haze I saw a 4,000-pound bag of ammonium nitrate that had burst wide open. Ammonium nitrate is the same blasting compound that Timothy McVeigh used to blow up the Alfred P. Murrah Building in Oklahoma City. The diamond mines use it for blasting. They put that ammonium nitrate down the hole, mixed with diesel fuel and a blasting cap, and—Boom!—it blows out huge sections of rocks the size of a couple of football fields. McVeigh had jammed 5,000 pounds into one van. I was carrying 160,000 pounds and now it was all over the ground in the middle of a smoking crash.

Hamilton was nowhere to be seen.

He had popped the axles off his trailer, and that had caused his rig to jackknife 90 degrees out. There was a snowdrift 20 feet high that had been bladed aside to open the road. Hamilton's trailer leveled it flat. I was in pain but not injured, so I kicked open my door and scrambled out to discover that

Hamilton's truck had creased my diesel tank, which contained 150 gallons of fuel. When I saw that, my eyes snapped back over to the open bag of explosive compound now running out onto the ice. Ammonium nitrate melts ice worse than salt. It was melting straight through. I grabbed a tarp from my cab and started shoveling ammonium nitrate onto the tarp as fast as I could. I shoveled and scooped like a madman. It might have been 10 degrees out, but I was cursing and sweating bullets.

I always carry duct tape and haywire, just in case, so I duct-taped the bag up until somebody came rushing up with a truck. They brought another bag—empty, this time—and we worked together to rig the bag up to collect the ammonium nitrate. The other guy had a front-end loader, thank God, so we tipped the broken bag into the new bag and got it off the ice as quickly as possible. It was blind chance that the truck came with a loader. If I had been hurt, that whole bag would have been on the ice, and the whole load—truck, explosives, and all—would have gone down through the ice and into the lake, taking me with it.

When Hamilton hit me, I was sure that I was finished. In the end, all I did was hurt my thumb. Hamilton finally got out of his truck, the son of a bitch. I wanted to kill him, but fig-ured eventually the ice roads would do it for me. He was fired instead. Hamilton's old man had four trucks on the ice roads, so he had some pull, but this accident was his fourth of the season and that finished him off. A guy like that doesn't be-long on the roads.

That final week is the last gasp of winter. Spring is in high gear and it's getting warm. There's fog coming up from the lakes. The ice is flooded with water, but it's self-healing, so all the cracks are filled to the point where it's just like gleaming crystal glass. The texture is smooth and clear. For the first time all season you can see through the ice to some 40 feet down. Right there is the reef structure and hints of current that you catch when the light is just right. You can see fish swimming around too: 40-pound trout. For the past month or so, I've come to think of the winter road as invincible, but now the black ice is gone. That trout is a sign as sure as the sound of the tick-tock of a bastard clock that tells me that we are on borrowed time.

The ice is gorgeous, but it's not the kind of ice you want to drive on. Not only is it slick, it's spongy, too. The weight of your load shifts from side to side like a kid's bounce house. You want the ugly black ice that your tires can grab at and get traction on. Not this. This is like playing ice hockey wearing roller skates.

People will tell you that you're crazy going out when the roads are like that, but I'm not going to let a bit of spongy ice stop me. I just want to get the job done.

Nobody's just going to give it to you, right?

I've seen ice road seasons that ended as early as late March. Other times, we keep going strong right up to mid-April. It all depends on the temperature. Things start heating up and the ice starts melting. Especially at the end of the year, I've broken through the ice and fallen in the water

Place of Man

lots of times. The ice is starting to break up along the shoreline, which is the weakest part of the road. Along comes a truck that crashes right through. Fortunately, the water is shallow. Often, you're partially on the ground, so it's not deep enough to lose the truck, but then you're stuck and need a tow.

By the end of the year, we're driving in water up on our tires about a foot deep. It looks worse than it is. The ice is still good but the texture is straight glass. You can't scuff it with a grader because it floods every day and freezes mirror-smooth every night. The ice is so thick that it doesn't matter even if the top 12 inches all melt. As a matter of fact, you can go up there in May and June and fly over the ice roads, and you'll see that the tracks are still frozen. Everything else might be melted but those two tracks that the trucks were riding on are still there. Sometimes they'll still be there until the freeze-up the next fall. It'll be July, and you'll see chunks of ice floating where the tracks were going. The year we had 12,000 loads go up, the ice measured 7 feet thick because so many trucks drove over it.

When you drive at the end of the season, the water bubbles up and flows fast like a river all around you. Once the water starts running, it will eat away at the top ice like rust on metal. That's when you know it's time to go home.

Rookies aren't allowed to drive at the end of the season because they wouldn't know what to do when the water is running. A lot of them might panic, unsure of which sections of road are still safe.

Four winters ago we had to wait for the ice to freeze up.

We might haul for a couple days when it got cold, then it would warm right up again, and the water would start running. We had to put wooden bridges over holes in the lake. Say there's a shoal going across a lake so it's shallow. Of course, when you're pushing on that, the wave comes up. The ice is so thin there that the wave busts it wide open. So we have to put wooden bridges down. After they're in place, then you'd get up on the bridge with your loads, going across at 3 miles an hour. All of a sudden you've got a hundred trucks hauling, and everybody's backed up on different portages. They'd radio, "Okay, you can come by." It made for a really long winter. Say your round trip usually takes thirty-six hours. Now you're up to forty-four hours.

A washout is where the water has been running across the road. It's washed out. Now either you've got to build another road—actually blade a new road—or put a bridge across. Just a couple years ago, we had seven of us going up. All of us were ice road veterans and we knew it was our last trip for the season. So we rode up together in a single convoy. Already, the lakes were open, the water was running all around, and the ice was crumbling away in chunks. But those final loads are your chance to make some good money. I'd say "easy money," but there's nothing easy about it that late in the season. So we tried our luck, but not one of us made it. There was one bad spot right around portages 22 and 23. The water always starts running early there, and if it's a warm year, it runs all year round.

Seven of us got up there with loads and we just had to keep pulling each other out. All the way through the run, we'd hook on and pull each other out. We'd get one guy out and the next guy would go in, and we'd pull him out. That was the only way to do it. If you keep your head on straight, you'll be fine. It sounds funny to say, but at that time of the year, you're battling the elements. When things go wrong, you can blame Mother Nature. When it's all frozen up and everything is going good, it's mostly pretty much human error.

A couple years ago, a guy went down right in front of me. He was a little close to the edge, but it was still the road. It was still where it was plowed, but it was a thin spot, and his truck just went down. They do an investigation every time, and it was ruled that it wasn't his fault. It was ruled that it was the road. They investigate everything and they know who's at fault, for sure.

The same year that my brother-in-law Paul and I had made the run on the Denison Road to Salmita, we took one of the last loads up to Diavik, right before they decided whether to close the roads. Leading the way with Paul half a mile behind, I came to a section of ice where we were between a rock and a hard place. A torrent of water was running hard on one side, and you could see great big chunks of ice breaking away. I went out to check the middle section of road to the right of the running water that looked okay from a distance but I had my doubts as I got closer. Sure enough, spongy as hell. Put your weight down, and an imprint of your boot would remain. I shuddered to think what would happen to a truck on the same spot.

That just left the right shoulder of the road, which gleamed like glass in the sun. In the ice, you could see not only yourself but also the clouds passing overhead. I climbed back into the Crow's Nest and came on. Traction wasn't worth a damn, but as long as you didn't brake and just kept a slow, steady pace, you would be okay. As soon as I had made it through fine, I called Paul behind me.

"Stay hard to the right," I said. "That's the only way to do it."

I had to keep moving and couldn't stop to see how Paul made out.

"I'm stuck," came Paul's voice over the radio.

"Shit. Whereabouts?"

"Where do you think? Right smack in the goddamn middle of that sorry-ass patch you warned me about. I'm spinning wheels here."

"All right. Hold tight. Lemme figure something out."

I called in for a hover vehicle to go back to see where he was. Well, by this time, there was water running everywhere, up over the tires in places. I wasn't more than a quarter-mile ahead of Paul, so I got out to walk back to give Paul a hand. I went about 20 feet before going ass over teakettle right on my back. Damn, that water was cold. Even though the water was running, it was still 30 below.

I had to get back in the truck right away and tell security what had happened.

"The goddamn road is turning to shit and my partner is stranded and I can't get near him."

I made the call, then had to get out of my clothes as quickly as possible, because everything I was wearing was frozen stiff and I was in danger of ending up the same way. I couldn't bend my arms or legs. I changed into my coveralls and got out again to try to help Paul.

I drove my truck up to where I knew they had a Sno-Cat, parked on the portage. Sno-Cats are lightweight vehicles that run on tracks, which gives them superior traction in these kinds of situations. I climbed into the vehicle and raced back to Paul.

He was waiting patiently but had that look on his face that said, "Well, here's another fine mess you've gotten me into, Chumley."

"Good day for a swim, anyway," I said. No sooner were the words out of my mouth than BAM!—right back into the water I went. Cursing and spitting fire, I pulled myself out. By the time I made it back to the truck, I moved about as well as Robocop. I had to blast the heater just so that I could bend and take my coat off along with everything else.

Finally, I called down to dispatch.

"We can't make her," I said. "Don't send anybody else up. You've got to close the roads."

The winter roads were officially closed, and since we couldn't turn around, we had to continue on and finish the run with or without security. Somehow we made it through. We had to leave our rigs at the mine. They sat for nine months waiting for me to come back. We couldn't get out the way we came, so we had to fly out. You would think we were able to finally breathe easy, but you would be wrong. By the time the plane was ready to take us, we were trying to beat one last thumb in the eye from Mother Nature. A storm was coming in.

"We'll be fine," the pilot said.

It was just a hop and a skip back to Yellowknife, but all the way, Paul and I were rocking and rolling and bouncing around. The little plane was practically falling out of the sky as much as we were going straight. But hell, we made it.

I learned a long time ago that no two last days are alike. You just have to focus on the ice and make it home safe. That was never truer than in the season of 1998.

Nuna Logistics controls the road, and at the end of 1998, they were saying the ice was closed pending further review. That meant that the roads were closed for traffic, but there were several high-priority loads that had just arrived from Edmonton and had yet to be delivered. If it didn't happen now, the mines would be forced to wait at least nine months for the ice roads to open the following year. Sometimes the ice will break up and that will be that. Game over. Other times, depending on the weather and recent conditions, the ice can self-heal and if you're patient, you might be able to get a few more loads in. Patty, the dispatcher at Tli Cho, told me:

"We're going to wait to see if the ice freezes up again, and if it does, anybody who is left will go together for one last haul. There's no guarantee that there will be another run, so you can go home if you want to."

"You guys know me better than that," I said. "Matter of fact, I'm ready to go now. I think the roads will hold. I can be back before everybody is loaded. Reg and I are willing to try for it."

"No, no," was the answer. "As it stands, the roads are closed."

I wanted the extra load, not just because it was the last one of the season but also because I needed a new track loader and they cost $70,000. Some people call them crawl-dozers, and whatever you want to call it, I needed one for my summer work. Track loaders are versatile and handy on a job site. Like me, they're jacks of all trades but masters of none. So there was something on the line for me in getting this last run in. I always get the first loads up and the last loads out. You get a $100-a-load bonus from the mines for every load you haul. So I have four trucks. You haul a hundred loads up, that's $10,000. Two hundred loads, that's a $20,000 bonus.

I don't like waiting, but I had no choice. For fourteen hours, I kept an eagle eye on the thermometer and waited in town to see what was going to happen. I couldn't sleep or re-lax. Finally, I got a call from Patty.

"Okay, one last load. Seven trucks. Hugh, you're ready so you're going to lead it." I was hoping to go solo with my buddy Reggie, like I had all season, but now I'm leading a team. Not just any team but most of the main guys, all-star drivers ev-ery one of them, including Alex, Jay Westgard, Mike, Roman, and Shawn.

Besides Reg and me, there were seven of us ready to roll, but the word goes out: "One last load. They're going for one last load." Other drivers want to get in on it. I guess they fig-ured, safety in numbers. Well, they kept adding trucks to the convoy, so by the time we got going, we had fourteen veteran drivers, including aces Carl and Ben willing to test their luck on what were likely to be the trickiest roads of the season.

Meanwhile, Reg and I had been up for eighteen hours straight and we hadn't even started yet.

"Well, looks like we got a dozen cowboys here to join us," says Reg.

"We'll be fourteen cowboys . . . Or fourteen head of cattle headed for slaughter, we'll soon find out," I answer. "Either way, I mean to keep my end up."

Finally, we were underway down the Igraham Trail. We made it to the Meadows.

I took a deep breath and blew it out, just relieved to be on the ice. We were fighting the ice the whole way, but we were doing okay, all things considered. When the ice is slick like that, you've got to be careful about everything you do. No quick movements, just steady, slow, and easy. Plan every move you make ahead of time. Meanwhile, steam is rising all around so thick that you can hardly see. We call this "ice fog." Tree lines and everything around you is bleary and in a soft focus that glows with halos of orange light when the sun hits it just right. The ice fog would be beautiful if we weren't in the middle of it.

We'd been on the road for eight hours by this time, which meant that we'd been up for twenty-four hours. Reggie was directly behind me, but he was getting tired. I could just tell. I tried to keep him awake by talking on the radio, but he dozed off in mid-sentence and slammed into the snowbank with his full load.

Shit.

Security is on the radio, just listening for these kinds of situations. If they hear something they don't like (every time a truck goes into a snowbank, there's supposed to be an investigation), they might cancel the run.

There was no time to waste; we all knew that. I had to get Reg out of there. We were losing the ice. Fast. I get on the radio and say, "Go up to channel 13450." I was directing him to my private frequency. Security operates on just two channels and doesn't have the higher frequencies.

When a truck gets stuck, we're ready with big tow straps rated for 160,000 pounds. You can put two super-Bs back to back, then go and hit it as hard as you can, and the strap will pull it out like a rubber band. The last guy in the convoy goes to step out to help Reg, but the ice is slick as snot. It's just crystal glass with a little glaze of water on it with the sun glaring off of it. He can't even stand up. He literally can't stand upright, let alone walk. He has to crawl his way over to Reg's truck.

"What in the world have we got ourselves into?" I hear Alex say over the radio several times.

"It can't all be cake, now can it?" I answer back.

So we get the big strap out, pull Reg out and dust him off, and away we go. I ask Reg if he's okay to run and he tells me he is. Now I'm sitting there waiting for everybody, because I'm ahead, so I have to wait for Alex, who pulled Reg out. I'm tired, but I'm talking on the radio to keep things running smooth. All of my joints have that bone-on-bone feeling. The palms of my hands feel raw in the cold and burn in the heat of the cab. I'm a little light-headed but trying to focus on the radio and what everyone else is doing, so that at first I don't realize that I'm sliding. I start to nod off and miss the portage altogether and go right off the edge of the lake to crash into a snowbank. Truthfully, I don't know whether I'm asleep or awake. So now another truck has to come pull me out. They pull me out. I shake the cobwebs out of my head and off we go.

Meanwhile, I can't get Reg on the radio. Turns out, he's pulled over and is sleeping in his truck. We've been going almost twenty-six hours straight and the glare off the ice cuts you right down. I'm about ready to join him on the rack but I hate giving up. I hate it. Back me in a corner and I will claw my way out. It's what I know. No way am I not going to see this through. I'm hollering at Reg, "We gotta go!" Alex finally has to go to Reg's truck and wake him up. We're on our way again. Reg makes it over to the portage onto the next lake, but then he hits the ditch and immediately falls asleep. This is all within an hour and a half. We pull him out again and are finally on the way. The lake we're on normally takes about an hour and forty-five minutes to cross. We're about twenty minutes up the lake when somebody else hits the ditch. At this rate, we'll take hours. There's so much water everywhere that I can't hear the ice cracking.

That worries me.

"You keep going. I'll go back for this guy," I say. Jay takes the lead. Instead of everybody coming up and getting the strap, I just make a big circle on the ice road. Some of these patches are in a hell of a bad shape, but every gut instinct I've ever had tells me they'll hold. If I'm wrong, well, I don't fucking care. Me, the ice, and the guys—we're all in this together.

The ice keeps its promise and holds me up. Now I'm in the rear. I hook up Reg's truck and pull him out. Now I'm in the back and Reg is leading. It's crazy, I know. We're all a little crazy at this point, but somehow we all make it to the end of the lake and are about to come off onto a portage when another truck misses the portage access and goes into the snowbank.

After that, it starts to really get ridiculous. Guys are sliding right off the roads and into the snow left and right. We're just leapfrogging everybody who is getting pulled out. By now, we'd been up thirty-six hours, white-knuckle ramming and slamming our way across the ice. We're fried. I get so I can't keep my eyes open. They hurt like hell. It's all going to hell but we stick at it, keep talking to each other—keep pulling each other out. After a while, I lost track of how many times we hit the ditch. With so many trucks, it has to be at least nine. But this is the last load and people are counting on us. That's what I keep telling everybody. The ice has to hold and we just have to stay awake to get up there. Nobody is going to let anybody down. Because there are fourteen of us, we keep pushing each other and somehow we all make it. By the time we get back, we'd been up more than fifty-four hours straight. My vision is all blurry. I feel like I'm half blind, half drunk. My whole body aches but I'm laughing. The guys look at me and each other like we're waking from some crazy dream. We can hardly believe that we're on solid ground. Jesus Christ, we've done it. Six hundred drivers started this journey and ten thousand loads later, it's just down to us. At least for today, everything else is cake.

"Well, that sure as hell is one trip to tell the grandkids," I croak out, realizing that somewhere along the way I lost my voice. I see a range of happiness, astonishment, and weariness on the faces of my friends and the other drivers.

"You're goddamn right about that, Hoodoo! Fourteen cowboys," says Reg.

I must be half out of my mind, but with that crazy French Canadian accent of his, Reg's voice sounds like the most hilarious, most wonderful thing I've ever heard. I roar with laughter and slam my hand into his.

"Yippie ki-yay!" I shout.

I turned in my paperwork. For a second, it felt very strange to have nothing in my chapped hands except my gloves. Ten weeks ago, I had made a promise to myself and to my family and now it was a promise kept. Now it was time to go. I returned to my truck, where I grabbed my bag and locked her up for when I would return in nine months.

A freight plane waited to take us to the airport, where we would head on home. I climbed in and took my seat. Some of the guys were already in there, but we were all talked out. A couple of them were asleep and the rest were rummaging through bags for tickets and confirmations. Their minds were on whatever came next. As the plane lifted higher and higher, I peered down at the ice road snaking across the tundra below. It was as fragile as a thread. I felt as if I were seeing it for the first time. Beyond the road, I saw where the water was rising, already poised to reclaim all that it rightfully owned.

All too soon I will start missing that goddamn ice and dream about the hurly-burly road, and I will start making my plans to get back, but not today and not tonight.

Man, it will be good to hug Dianne.

EPILOGUE

To me, the ice roads are about freedom and independence. You can work as hard as you want and you're free to build your own future. Of course, you're also free to freeze to death if you're not careful. I guess that's the flip side. Too many times, people say they want the first but aren't willing to risk the second. Working on the ice roads isn't about having an adventure just so you can say you had an adventure. Anybody can risk his neck for no good reason. Trucking in the Arctic is about doing a dangerous job because that's the opportunity you were given to put good money in your pocket to feed your family and keep a roof over your head. If that means being away from your wife and kids for a few months, well, that's what it is. The ice roads are about working as hard as you ever did in your life and having something to show for it. If there's a little adventure mixed in there someplace, well, that's fine by me.

I'm proud of what I do for a living. The saying goes, "If you bought it, a trucker brought it." Whatever you can imagine, I've hauled it. Over the years, I've worked with hundreds of drivers. Most of them are spread around Canada. Only a few, like my buddy Reg, do I call in the off-season. Without the ice to bond us, most of us don't have much in common. Some have moved on from the ice roads. Others have died right in their trucks. Driving the winter road is a stressful life. It's not easy to stay healthy, and heart attacks are common. If it happens out on the ice, you're far from help. After a while, you forget their names but remember their faces.

I've given the ice road the best years of my life and I truly believe that it has reciprocated in kind. I've crashed and survived. Anything that's worth doing involves risk, and either you're living or you're dead. We only get one kick at the cat. Every single day, no matter how rich or important you are, everybody gets the same twenty-four-hour clock. It's what you do with it that makes the time different. I like to think I've done pretty okay with mine.

Given all the wrecks and tough situations I've been in, some people have thought I'd never make it out of my younger days—my own mother, for instance. When the time comes, the time comes, I guess. In the meantime, I'll keep at it. I'll run the run on the ice as long as I can. When my reflexes give out and the cold gets to be too much, then my time will be done.

I can see a time when there won't be any more winter roads. Not because of climate change or global warming, but because of the economics. Ice roads are expensive to build. They're always working on cheaper ways to deliver the things people need up there. It's just a matter of time. Within ten years from now, the time of the ice roads will be over. A few years ago, work began on a port on the Mackenzie Bay. Now, they have proposed building a 125-mile high-grade all-weather road from Bathurst to Contwoyto. If they do that, the ice roads will be done. Companies will be able to haul down from the Mackenzie Bay all year round. Jobs like mine will become relics of history, like the dogsled teams of the last century that were once the only lifeline in the Arctic.

Someday, you'll say that you used to drive a truck over ice and people will think you're crazy. The next generation won't even know what people are talking about unless they read about it. I'll say, "Back in '85 or '97, when we used to haul up on the ice roads to the diamond mines . . ." and people will say, "What are you talking about? What do you mean, traveling on ice?" It will sound like a strange story.

Even the Mackenzie River crossing is almost history. A bridge is under construction and scheduled for completion by 2015. When there's a bridge across Mackenzie, the crossing and the ferry will be obsolete. When that happens, the North will open up to everyone and change completely. Even the cold won't hold people back forever—not when there's so much money to be made. That's just human nature. Still, I'm glad to have played my part. I feel like all of us who drive every day of the season and have gone above and beyond what we were expected to do are playing our part in the making of history. The ice roads prove that this world is still full of opportunities. You just have to go out and get them. Don't look for a light load. Instead, get yourself a strong back.

Head down, ass up, and carry on.

SELECTED BIBLIOGRAPHY

Gow, Sandy and Bonar Alexander Gow. *Roughnecks, Rock Bits and Rigs: The Evolution of Oil Well Drilling in Alberta*. Calgary: University of Calgary Press, 2005.

Hamilton, John David. *Arctic Revolution: Social Change in the Northwest Territories, 1935–1994*. Toronto: Dundurn Press Limited, 1994.

Iglauer, Edith. *Denison's Ice Road*. New York: Dutton, 1975.

Selleck, Annette, Lee Selleck, and Francis Thompson. *Dying for Gold: The True Story of the Giant Mine Murders*. Toronto: HarperCollins, 1998.

Staples, David. *The Third Suspect*. Ontario: Red Deer College Press, 1995.

Wade, Frank. *Advocate for the North: Judge John Parker: His Life and Times in the Northwest Territories*. Victoria, BC: Trafford Publishing, 2004.